Dispatches
From Durban

Dispatches From Durban

Firsthand Commentaries on the
World Conference Against Racism
and
Post-September 11 Movement Strategies

Eric Mann

Frontlines Press

Frontlines Press

3780 Wilshire Blvd. Suite 1200

Los Angeles, California 90010

www.frontlinespress.com

To order copies of this book send $14.95 to the above address (in addition, please include $3 shipping and CA 8.25% sales tax) or go to www.frontlinespress.com

Portions of *Dispatches from Durban* originally appeared in AhoraNow Online Publications September 2001 www.ahoranow.org

Cover photo: Francis Calpotura "U.S. Stop Exporting Racism"

Cover design: Lian Hurst Mann

Text design: Geoff Ray

Printed in the United States of America

in memory of

Fannie Lou Hamer
Chris Hani
Joe Slovo
Ruth First

About the Author

Eric Mann is the director of the Labor/Community Strategy Center in Los Angeles. He has been a civil rights, anti-Vietnam war, labor, and environmental organizer for 35 years with the Congress of Racial Equality, the Students for a Democratic Society, the United Auto Workers, and the Bus Riders Union, including eight years on auto assembly lines. He was the lead organizer of the Labor/Community Campaign to Keep General Motors Van Nuys Open that stopped GM from closing the auto plant for ten years. He is a founding member of the Strategy Center and of the Bus Riders Union (BRU), sits on the BRU Planning Committee, and teaches at the Strategy Center's National School for Strategic Organizing.

He is the author of **Comrade George**: *An Investigation into the Life, Political Thought, and Assassination of George Jackson*; **Taking on General Motors**: *A Case Study of the UAW Campaign to Keep GM Van Nuys Open*; and **L.A.'s Lethal Air**: *New Strategies for Policy, Organizing and Action.*

Other Books by Eric Mann

COMRADE GEORGE: *An Investigation into the Life, Political Thought, and Assassintion of George Jackson*

"*Comrade George* is a passionate, yet, careful, analysis of the life and assassination of George Jackson. Its language is angry, but it subjects the official explanation of Jackson's death to a meticulous examination. More important, it connects the killings of Jackson to the current upsurge of revolt in the prisons. One cannot read this book without a feeling of outrage at the inhumanity of the system we live under. And yet, one also comes away with a sense of the possibilities that an ongoing struggle possesses for the future." **—Howard Zinn**

TAKING ON GENERAL MOTORS: *A Case Study of the UAW Campaign to Keep GM Van Nuys Open*

"I have marched with the Van Nuys UAW workers and observed their masterful organizing work first-hand. This complex case study of the construction of a successful labor/community movement to save L.A.'s last auto plant should be savored. If you are a labor or civil rights organizer, an environmental or peace activist, a college or high school teacher, or a member of the Rainbow Coalition, I urge you to read and distribute *Taking On General Motors* and creatively apply its many lessons to your own work." **—Rev. Jesse Jackson**

L.A.'S LETHAL AIR: *New Strategies for Policy, Organizing, and Action* (*El Aire Mortal de Los Angeles*)

"*L.A.'s Lethal Air* is a breath of fresh air; it translates cold environment statistics into a story about people. The chapter on "Class, Race, and Gender: The Unspoken Categories of Public Health" is a major breakthrough in environmental analysis. *L.A.'s Lethal Air* makes a unique, well-documented contribution to the environmental movement by placing responsibility for the devastating public health impacts of air pollution clearly at the feet of corporate America—and generating positive grassroots proposals for industrial and transportation policy." **—Barry Commoner**

Contents

Acknowledgements

I live in a collective context. Acknowledgments can hardly express the way I am supported and helped by so many friends and comrades; after all, we try to live the revolution in our daily lives.

Dispatches from Durban began through the invitation of Rinku Sen and Gary Delgado of the Applied Research Center in Oakland that permitted me to be part of their delegation to the World Conference Against Racism. I remain appreciative of such a great historical opportunity.

In South Africa I was given the gift of long conversations and even longer debates about the future. Thanks to Blade Nzimande, General Secretary of the South African Communist Party, Michael Sachs of the African National Congress, Mahlengi Bengu of the Congress of South African Trade Unions, Oupa Lehulere and Maria Van Trier of Khanya College, Godfrey Lenin Kgaphola from the SACP of Alexandra and Patrick Bond of University of Witwatersrand for their willingness to argue their case with integrity and their commitment to act on their own beliefs.

I am proud to be part of the Labor/Community Strategy Center and Bus Riders Union where I work with so many working class heroes, dedicated staff and members: Rosalio Mendiola, Maria Guardado, Woodrow Coleman, Shepherd Petit, Dan DiPasquo, Kirti Baranwal, Martin Hernandez, Ted Robertson, Manuel Criollo, Cynthia Rojas, Damon Azali, Robert Taylor, Alex Caputo-Pearl, Della Bonner, Norma Henry, Rita Burgos, Kikanza Ramsey, Daniel Widener, Rudy Pisani, Cirilo Juarez, Ricardo Zelada, Ruth Williams, Joe Itow, Carl Gunther, Joe Linton, Bianca Kovar, and Grandma Kim. Barbara Lott-Holland, the co-chair of the Bus Riders Union has provided energy, leadership, and an exemplary openness to new ideas. Kate Kinkade and Patrick Ramsey have been friends and board members since the Center's inception and provide a solid-as-a-rock backup for my work as director. Victor Wallis and Hoby Spalding have been comrades since the GM Van Nuys work and have always been in my corner.

Dispatches from Durban, the first book published by Frontlines Press, was produced by a collective of gifted people. Layla Welborn is a real talent, a very good-natured hard-liner, a dedicated friend of the Palestinian people, and an excellent project manager. Tammy Bang Luu researched all the facts with passion and great attention to detail. Angela Chung, an organizer-in-training, has raised proofreading to an art form. Deborah Orosz read each dispatch with great attention to political nuance. Geoff Ray is a close friend, master layout man, and fine business manager for our upstart press. Daniel Kim will be helping produce my next book *Revolutionary Organizing in the Age of Reaction.* Lian Hurst Mann, Ph.D., the doctor in the house, is my life partner and mentor; we are learning as we get older to enjoy the contention and debate that makes both of us stronger. Her overall editing on *Dispatches* took the form of strong political interventions that changed my mind at several key junctures and made the overall product a lot stronger.

Our daughters, Celia and Melinda, have grown up in L.A.'s public schools and now serve the inner city, Celia as a park director, Melinda as a new public school teacher. My mother-in-law, Melinda Hurst, has been a source of support and good humor for decades. My mom, Libby Mann, was the first person who taught me that Jews had to be antiracists, if the Holocaust was to mean anything. She made the connections between Jews and Blacks that have shaped so much of my life.

An organizer has to really like people, and I'm a very lucky person to have such great friends and comrades. We are making history together.

Foreword

Robin D. G. Kelley

The new millennium opened pretty disastrously. The 2000 presidential elections became virtually a coup d'etat for George Bush and the Republican Party, with the Supreme Court weighing in for the Right. So much for checks and balances. The Right's victory depended in part on the blatant disfranchisement of Black voters in Florida. The state circulated lists of alleged convicted felons—over 200,000 Black men in all. In Florida, as well as other states, convicted felons lose their right to vote. The list circulating at the polls was full of errors, and there was no mechanism to allow individuals to vote in the case of a mistaken identity. The fact that convicted felons, no matter what their crime, could lose their right to vote in perpetuity is already a problem; that innocent individuals were also denied the vote should have been considered egregious to anyone who claimed to believe in democracy. But there was little outcry beyond the usual suspects.

As a result, we now have Bush in the White House and John Ashcroft as head cop in charge. The wholesale repression of political dissidents is neither a past memory nor the stuff of conspiracy-prone science fiction. It's here. The rapaciousness of corporations on a global scale, the erosion of a safety net for the poor, the increase in homelessness, the growing number of people unable to obtain medical insurance, the impending reversal of *Roe v. Wade*, the wholesale destruction of the environment, and a host of other issues are making living difficult—not just for people in the U.S. but throughout the world. The so-called capitalist miracle in the 1990s is turning out to be quite a scam. The future of capitalism is on shaky grounds right now.

Dispatches from Durban analyzes the current crisis with the goal of building a vibrant antiracist, anti-imperialist Left. While Eric Mann is optimistic enough to believe that a broad left challenge to capitalism, racism, and imperialism is possible—indeed, necessary—his portrait of the condition of the world is bleak, to say the least. Under the Bush administration's global war, he argues, we are witnessing the suppression of self-determination for nations of the Global South and the real possibility of recolonization; massive poverty and the disappearance of viable welfare states in the face of structural adjustment policies; privatization of the commons, resulting in "imperialist penetration and control over indigenous resources"; unbridled corporate destruction of the environment resulting in global warming, disastrous weather events, droughts and epidemics; and the suppression of radical movements for social justice and transformation.

Times are rough but, rather than mourn, Eric Mann and his comrades at the Labor/Community Strategy Center and the Bus Riders Union set out to organize. *Dispatches from Durban* is not a blueprint for revolution, but it is a strategic document. Mann, after all, is an organizer first and foremost. A veteran of the civil rights, environmental justice, and labor movements, he has been a major voice on the revolutionary Left for nearly four decades. Given his history, it is not an accident that *Dispatches* was largely produced in Durban, South Africa, during his participation in the historic World Conference Against Racism (WCAR). The Durban conference was a critical world-historical event, something akin to our generation's Bandung—the conference of Non-Aligned Nations in Indonesia in 1955. In some ways, WCAR was a victory for progressive forces, but it also laid bare the weakness of the U.S. Left and the global antiracist, anti-imperialist movement. On the one hand, the U.S. delegation's decision to walk out of WCAR because it could not suppress discussion of Israel's oppression of the Palestinians or reparations for Africa and its descendants was, in many ways, a defeat for the U.S. On the other hand, the debate over Israel and reparations also exposed the weaknesses of the U.S. Left. As Mann reports, some delegates complained that Arab delegates "hijacked" the conference and that the Palestinian question deflected attention from issues like reparations. Although in the end there was more unity than division around these burning issues, the failure to see how these struggles are inextricably linked underscores a political myopia that has been plaguing U.S. progressive forces for some time now.

Dispatches from Durban addresses the Left's slow retreat from internationalism. Especially in light of the tragedy of September 11th and its aftermath, we are finding an increasing number of U.S. Leftists supporting the war in Afghanistan and voicing their support for a left patriotic culture. Mann questions whether it is even possible for internationalists to stand behind any national flag, particularly the stars and stripes, because it has come to represent a long history of intervention, warmongering, and imperialism. Moreover, embracing patriotism makes it difficult to build international solidarity and oppose U.S. imperialism in other parts of the world.

Mann addresses the separation between the anti-globalization movement and the antiracist and reparations movements. Indeed, if we go back just two decades, we are reminded that what is now called anti-globalization was considered anti-imperialist. In the 1980s we lived through a period of tremendous right-wing drift, capital flight, monopolization, unemployment, decline of urban communities, and state terror, but the movements that emerged in opposition created real challenges for the Right. It was the age when a vibrant anti-Apartheid movement helped bring about an end to white minority rule in South Africa. Solidarity movements in support of struggles for justice in Central America, Africa, and Asia were very active and visible. Some of these movements were sustained by new immigrants, many of whom were refugees of what Commandante Marcos calls the "Third World War"—the last half century of U.S. intervention, counterinsurgency missions, Cold War battles over control of the Global South, and revolutions. An unknown number of Salvadorans, Guatemalans, Mexicans, Grenadians, Haitians, South Africans, Sri Lankans, Koreans, etc., played critical roles in the resurgent anti-imperialist movements of the '80s. Mann understands these conditions well; influential political refugees of the era ended up in organizations such as the Labor/Community Strategy Center and the Bus Riders Union. In fact, the multinational character of the Bus Riders Union has everything to do with this particular generation of refugees from the "Third World War."

Mann insists that we need to revitalize a U.S. Left that can learn from the lessons of earlier anti-imperialist movements but develop strategies that are appropriate for our era. He imagines a Left capable of blocking U.S. intervention in Third World countries, battling corporate globalization, and defending the rights of oppressed nationalities here in the "belly of the beast." He calls on anti-globalization activists to take on racism as a central issue on a global as well as local level.

One crucial issue from the WCAR that worked to link racism and capitalism on a global scale is reparations for Africans and people of African descent. Mann highlights the reparations movement's revolutionary potential to expose the relationship between the development of capitalism, racism, colonialism and slavery. By claiming that a huge portion of accumulated capital was obtained illegitimately, arguments for reparations strike directly at institutions such as the World Bank, the IMF, the G8 nations and the U.S. itself. The demand for reparations, after all, is not for a hand-out but a down payment for centuries of unpaid labor, violence, and exploitation. Any effort to really come close to making a just retribution would "break the bank," so to speak. Finally, a successful reparations campaign can also transform the lives of many struggling working people, not just people of African descent. Assuming that reparations would be paid out to institutions rather than to individuals, it would mean that all impoverished urban residents would benefit from a massive

infusion of capital for infrastructure, housing, schools, civic organizations, and related institutions. Demanding such a transfer
of resources makes perfect historical sense because the large
populations of Latinos, Native Americans, and Asian Americans
who occupy poor urban communities are products of centuries
of imperialism—slavery's handmaiden, if you will. And obviously,
Afro-Caribbean immigrants to the U.S. are also descendants of
slaves and products of policies that compelled them to leave
one kind of poverty for another.

As *Dispatches from Durban* makes clear, Mann's actual
experience with the Left in South Africa profoundly shapes
the ideas and tenor of this book. Marching in the streets of
Durban with African workers in solidarity with the Congress
of South African Trade Unions, Mann recognized immediately
that the South African Left has many lessons to teach radicals in the United States about building strategic alliances.
The critical yet fragile alliance between the South African Communist Party, the African National Congress, and the labor
movement exposes just how difficult it is for socialists to hold
state power in a capitalist world. President Thabo Mbeki's
move toward greater privatization has resulted in greater suffering among working people. Yet, as Mann shows us, unlike
the United States, the South African Left is strong, the unions
are well organized and militant, and there is an unusually high
level of debate and political participation throughout the country.
South African Leftists know that they must walk a fine line
as both critics and supporters of the regime, for the threat of
intervention always looms overhead. Whether it is Guatemala,
or Chile, or Grenada, they know the history of imperialist
intervention all too well.

The South African Left's ability to survive and even shape state politics is an amazing, inspiring example. But the most important lesson the struggle there can teach us is how bloody difficult it is to imagine and realize a new society. Different factions are trying to do the impossible work of reconstruction and reconciliation in the midst of internal wars and international capitalist pressures. In many ways, *Dispatches from Durban* speaks to the same condition of urgency, the same kind of immediacy that can force us to respond to crises before we have a chance to map out a different future. Don't get me wrong; it is a strategic imperative to defend our lives, the earth, and our right to dissent, thus, to challenge neoliberalism, racism, and imperialism.

My sister, Makani Themba, also attended the WCAR and also came away with a sense that something new was being built on an international scale. And yet, in her own "Durban Diary" she was haunted by the fundamental question of how to struggle for a new society, especially given the suffering she witnessed all around her. "It is far easier to organize *against* a common enemy than *for* a common vision," she wrote a couple days before returning home. "South Africa knows there are few examples of how to build a nation where everyone is truly free. Making sure people have enough to eat, have a roof over their heads, and enough space in their lives for love and laughter are not the rousing stuff of songs."

Here is the other reason why the revitalized radical movement Mann imagines is so important. We need to think beyond the immediate crises and begin to talk about the future again. Socialists, utopian and scientific, always had the best dreams because they fought to create a space where there is no want of necessities and there would be "enough space in their lives for love and laughter." Even in a place as ravaged as South Africa, grassroots radicals, like Eric Mann's local guide 'Lenin,' are working to create a new culture in the townships, one of cooperation and community. It is precisely this sort of work we need if we are going to transform our war zones into "liberated zones." A revitalized Left can never sustain itself without this broader vision of what we want to build and what is possible.

Mann envisions a renaissance for the Left. There is a refreshing, at times startling, realpolitik optimism running throughout this book.

—Robin D. G. Kelley
Professor of History and Africana Studies
New York University

Introduction

Home is where the heart is, and for me, the heart is where the organizing is. I am a grassroots organizer; it's in my blood. I stay close to low-income communities—Black and Latino communities where I have lived, worked, and organized most of my life. I stay close to auto, electronics, restaurant, and hospital workers, among whom I have spent much of my life as bus boy and waiter, nurses aide and operating room orderly, electronic assembler and auto worker. I have come to hate big business from my "labor relations" education at Cornell, my exposure to radical books, films, and organizers, and from first hand experience. I have worked for some of the biggest U.S. transnationals—IBM, Ford and General Motors—twelve years as an assembly line worker, getting a good view of corporate capitalism from the bottom up. As I came to understand the U.S. as an empire, my greatest hope in the fight against imperialism has always been the organization of oppressed peoples.

I don't travel regularly to international conferences. There is always something so compelling in the day-to-day struggle against the system that makes it seem like the struggle of the century. Sometimes it is, often it is not, but my sense that every tactic, no matter how small, is essential to the ultimate victory or defeat of a particular campaign has been a hallmark of my work, and a key to many victories I have helped to win against far more powerful adversaries. That attention to daily detail makes it hard for me to remember that my trips to participate in political gatherings in Mexico, Italy, Canada, Germany and China have always been so influential in my development. After 35 years of organizing I should listen to my own words— I often tell others who worry about taking time away to attend an international meeting "Don't worry, I promise you that the racism and imperialism will still be here when you get back, and if we solve it while you're gone we'll be sure to give you a call."

So last July, I get a phone call from Rinku Sen, formerly of the Center for Third World Organizing and now on the staff of its sister project, the Applied Research Center (ARC), "We have one more opening on our delegation, you have to decide today, do you want to go to South Africa for the World Conference Against Racism?" Did I? What a question. I called my wife Lian, and said "I have to decide in an hour. Should I go—is it okay on the home front?" "Of course it's okay, Eric. It's great. Go for it," she tells me. We have always encouraged each other to take advantage of every political opportunity; still, it's great to go with support from your best friend. It was also very generous of Rinku and Gary Delgado from ARC. We talk of solidarity in the movement, but it's hard to get. As a white,

Jewish organizer, I was particularly honored to have been invited, and I am so grateful for what turned out to be a transformative experience.

I decided from the beginning to go as a journalist as well as an organizer. I love to write, and used to make a living at it, covering the prison movement and the world for the Boston *Realpaper* and *Boston After Dark* in the early 1980s. It would be fun to be a left reporter again, well, not a reporter, a commentator, for no one is neutral. I decided to write "dispatches" from Durban and put out my views through the magic of the Internet and email listserves.

The Strategy Center, my political home, is also the scene of my best friends and comrades. Lian had been planning to have two weeks for herself while I was in South Africa, only to come to realize, when I asked for her help, that "my" dispatches from Durban would become "our" project. She is a great editor, all of our work over decades has been influenced by each other, and there was no way I could write stuff right on the spot in a country I had never been in about a conference I had never attended without at least one thoughtful comrade on the other end of the world, to provide ballast and counterweight to any ideas from the frontlines. She agreed to help with all the rewrites that would be needed as the stuff came hot off the internet. Her editorial and political hand is obvious throughout, but, in particular, on the COSATU (Congress of South African Trade Unions) march article where her rewrites helped to shape my approach toward the work to follow, which has now become this book. Having served as editor of her work as well, I know the rare excitement of a personal political partnership.

Then Geoff Ray, the Center's administrator, agreed to give up his Labor Day vacation to produce the dispatches, get them up on listserves. I sent out my first dispatch before I left for South Africa ("On to Durban: Putting the Heat on the U.S.," Dispatch Number One), and the email responses I got back were beyond what I could have imagined, a multiracial but predominantly Black readership pushing me on, encouraging me to report back to them, more than 50 thoughtful emails just from the first dispatch, thus my sign off line on many of the dispatches, "I will keep you posted."

The key to the success of the writing project was the internet-based *Black Radical Congress News*, edited by Art McGee, which published all of my dispatches, and reached an amazing audience. This was supplemented by our own Strategy Center News list, as Geoff had created his own listserve of 400 or so key contacts, and ZNET, where Mike Albert helped us get out the word. It was strange being in South Africa, introducing myself to someone, and have them tell me, "Oh, Eric Mann, I just read your article last night." So here I am in the midst of 10,000 NGO delegates, I send a draft back to Lian, she edits it, Geoff puts it up on our website and sends it out on the listserves, and through the magic of the BRC, ZNET, and the Strategy Center, something I had written in Durban reappears back in Durban within a few hours and is read by a delegate who doesn't know me from Adam—or at least not until then. Those dispatches are read by a producer for Amy Goodman's path-breaking radio program *Democracy Now!*, who was in Durban with a broadcast crew, and the next day I am on Amy's show, radio-in-exile at the time, along with Mahlengi Bengu, Chief Education Officer of COSATU. So the multiplier effect continues. (The transcript of her interview is included after Dispatch 2—the "COSATU General Strike and the Treachery of the International Marketplace.")

As you will see from this book, I got very caught up in the debates about South African politics and the South African Left. It was quite an experience to listen to so many people disagree with each other (and disagreement I'm afraid is the order of the day in South Africa right now) at such a high level of theory. I have tried to convey the debates as best I can, giving each participant the fullest and fairest representation of their point of view. These are some very developed people, what a pleasure to be exposed to such a sophisticated level of political debate.

Walking on the beaches of Durban and the streets of Johannesburg, I had not understood before I arrived how beautiful South Africa is. The pain of thinking of how the European settlers stole it for centuries is even more intense when you see the country first hand. And the theft is far from over, even under Black majority rule. It was infuriating to watch so many South African whites, having so much money to spend, while the Blacks in South Africa, as a group, are still so poor. I remembered Amiri Baraka, the revolutionary poet, having said, "Why would the white folks ever give up capitalism voluntarily, for them, imperialism is heaven on earth." The question remains how the wretched of the earth can continue to rise up and make a new world.

Dispatches from Durban will pretty much speak for itself. By now you have read the jacket blurbs and read Robin Kelley's generous and insightful introduction. Some of you know who I am and know about my work. So just a few summaries of key arguments in the book and its objectives.

Dispatches situates itself within a world wide tendency that is trying to find some relationship, some synthesis, between Black revolutionary nationalism, anti-imperialism, and socialism.

Dispatches argues for the strategic centrality of the Black Liberation struggle inside the U.S. and the importance of a unified set of alliances among people of color. It also argues for the strategic importance of antiracist, and anti-imperialist whites, and within that grouping, the historical role of progressive and Left Jews in support of the Black movement, the Palestinian people, and the movements of Third World peoples inside and outside the U.S.

Dispatches places the U.S. government and U.S. imperialism squarely at the center of the world's problems and focuses on the building of an anti-imperialist united front as the key strategy for the world Left. At all times, antiracist politics is treated as effectively, or potentially, anti-imperialist. The World Conference Against Racism (WCAR) in Durban and the World Summit on Sustainable Development (WSSD) in Johannesburg are vibrant sites of contestation over these politics.

Dispatches views the South African Left as an advanced workshop for the world Left. I use the interviews with key South African intellectuals, organizers, and electoral leaders, not as a judgement as to what I think they should do, but as a way for those of us in the U.S. in particular to learn from and be challenged by a more advanced theory and practice.

Throughout *Dispatches,* I have had tried to address a fundamental contradiction between proposals for strategy and tactics and a movement that does not really exist, at least does not cohere, at this time in history. The book is fundamentally about strategy and tactics, and yet, strategy is very difficult to fathom, and impossible to implement without an organization. I consider myself very fortunate. I am part of two interrelated organizations—the Labor/Community Strategy Center and the Bus Riders Union—and from that base a series of major projects, the National School for Strategic Organizing, the Program Demand Group, AhoraNow publications, and now, Frontlines Press. I am also well aware of the limits of the Strategy Center, we exist to be part of a larger movement. And yet, at the national and international level, there is no organized form, no organized tendency, no caucus or network or political party that reflects my views or the proposals I am making in this book for a broader Left. Thus, throughout the book, the editors, Lian Hurst Mann and Layla Welborn, and I have been having trouble finding appropriate organizational references: "the multiracial Left in the U.S." (that does not yet exist), "the nascent world Left" (which often does not have any organized form, and whose component and constituent parts often are clear they do *not* want to work with each other) "the Black Liberation Movement" (which at this point in history would be difficult to bring under one roof, let alone one organization).

There is no question that one objective of this book is to help bring these forces together, to show the tremendous opportunities we had in Durban, in some ways (lets be honest) opportunities lost, in other ways, opportunities imagined and acted upon. I convey the movement victories in Durban, even if fleeting and transitory, to show the historical possibilities, and to challenge the white chauvinism and narrow nationalism, the individual and organizational competitiveness, and the fatal disease of sectarianism that has killed many a beautiful project in its infancy. *Dispatches* tries to combine the delineation of sharp political difference with a sense of generosity toward, and assumed good intentions of, many different forces on the Left. I want the book to be a tactic in a broader project of multiracial Left unity. We'll see how it goes.

In the section "Bringing It All Back Home," I write about the work of the Labor/Community Strategy Center as a hopeful, but hopefully not boastful, contribution to imagining what Left work can look like. It is hard for me to listen to people write articles or give speeches that say, "The Left should do this" or "We (whoever that is) must do that." I come out of a tradition of organizing: tell me what you are doing, why you are doing it, what you are building, the ups and downs of the work, and I can listen for hours. In that I do not speak for any broader Left than my own opinions and in some indirect ways my own organization, I wanted to give some examples of one organization whose director came back from Durban all fired up, and was able to convey that enthusiasm to a wonderful group of leaders who shared that view, and have acted upon it and collectivized the vision

The main audience for *Dispatches from Durban*, for the publications of the new Frontlines Press, is "the opinion leaders of the oppressed," the frontline organizers and activists in social movements, the welfare rights leaders and shop stewards, the activist professors and NGO militants, the people who others see as leaders, the people who get up in the morning to change the world, not just read about it and weep. I think we are talking about a lot of people now, and a whole lot more people in the future.

This prioritized audience is often overlaid with class and race and gender dynamics. That is, most working class women, most women of color who are involved in the movement or involved in a specific cause want to read books about how to fight, and how to win, and what should we do? This book is written for those who are angry and want to fight, and mainly those who are already fighting and those who, if I influence them, can influence others, for they are the opinion leaders of the oppressed.

I want to write for the largest audience possible, but the key audience that will actually move history. As such, I target Black readers, Latino readers, Asian/Pacific Islander readers, Indigenous peoples readers, Third World readers, women readers, and antiracist white readers. I am aware that the "movement" is not very big right now, but it is a lot bigger, if unfortunately dispersed, than people think.

I began my activism, my commitment to revolution, in 1964, when I went to work for the Congress of Racial Equality (CORE), a militant civil rights group at the time. By that time I had already joined the Civil Rights Movement, but many CORE veterans told me about their civil rights marches in the 1940s that were downright tiny, and the freedom rides in 1961, which had helped radicalize me when I was an audience, not an activist, let alone an organizer. They explained how step by step, year by year, they had gone from tiny to small and from small to mid-size and now in 1964 they had more members and more chapters than they knew how to handle. In 1965, George Wiley, my good friend and, at the time, deputy director of CORE sent me to represent the organization at a sit-in against Apartheid in South Africa staged at the Chase Manhattan Bank in New York's Wall Street district. And here I am still engaging the challenges of racism and South Africa today.

Perhaps I was hallucinating, but I swear I marched with millions of people during the 1960s who talked openly about racism and capitalism, women's liberation and socialism. But perhaps they all died and I didn't know it, or perhaps they have been invaded by the body snatchers, and they all have had a davidhorowitzectomy and repudiated everything they ever stood for or thought? I think not. I think the audience for this book is the hundreds of thousands (I want to say millions but that is, I'm afraid, wishful thinking) of veterans of the sixties and seventies who are not as radical as they once were, but still want to fight, to make a difference, and are open to being riled up and reorganized. At least I can try to reach them. But even more, I want to reach the tens of thousands of long-distance runners, who have kept their politics intact and are working in high schools teaching inner-city youth, or abortion clinics protecting women's right to choose, or serving as nurses at hospitals in urban medical centers fighting to keep people alive, or as trade union organizers or foundation officers or public interest or pro bono attorneys fighting the rich and fighting for the poor.

And what of the youth? Am I hallucinating again, because I see them, the Blacks and Latinos, the Asian/Pacific Islanders and antiracist whites, fighting against sweatshops and globalization, organizing in communities of color against police violence, mobilizing immigrants and welfare mothers, planning union organizing drives and demanding a living wage, challenging the International Monetary Fund and World Trade Organization, writing great stuff on the endless listserves on which geniuses, madmen and madwomen coexist. Even at a point of Left disorientation with no national or international socialist or communist project, there are tens of thousands of these people, no hundreds of thousands of them at least, who know something is very rotten in this country, who see through George Bush and the Democrats with the greatest of ease, who will vote for Nader and the Greens or not vote at all, will march against the World Bank and risk their lives as the post-September 11 police state talks about "shoot to kill."

They will pass up a corporate job for a community one. Thousands of young public school teachers experience first hand how the U.S. lets its public schools rot in hell and subjects the students and teachers to a robot-like standardized testing, while diverting public education funds, in the form of school vouchers, to Christian fundamentalist schools. No, I am revising my estimate, it's over a million people I bet who consider themselves active, activists, organizers, left liberals, progressives, radicals, socialists, revolutionaries, antiracists, anti-globalization activists, anti-imperialist organizers. They like Fidel Castro and don't like George Bush, they care about the Global South and are truly ashamed of U.S. society with its avarice, racism, and arrogance. And they want to fight back, they're looking for a strategy. They want to make a difference. If only "the movement" could come back, they would march and picket and sit-in and even risk their lives, if there was an organization, if only there was a clear plan.

Dispatches from Durban is not a revolutionary manifesto, although I am working on one, *Revolutionary Organizing in the*

Age of Reaction. But *Dispatches* is a strategic document that contains the seeds of a broader Left strategy, the antiracist, anti-imperialist united front, a positive vision of a society, organizing to stop the abuses of the existing system. *Dispatches from Durban* lays out a framework for a broader strategic vision, and provides plenty of suggestions for immediate tactical interventions. One of the last dispatches, "Bulletin from Bali," ends with the central question facing all of us, "What are *You* Going to Do About the United States?"

For those who are already asking that question, all over the world, you are my audience.

Eric Mann
July 31, 2002

August 23, 2001
LOS ANGELES

On to Durban:
Putting the Heat on the U.S.

This Saturday, I leave for the United Nations World Conference Against Racism (WCAR) in Durban, South Africa, as part of a multiracial delegation initiated by the Applied Research Center. If this were 1955, at the historic conference of Non-Aligned Nations in Bandung, Indonesia, or 1965, after the passage of the Civil Rights and the Voting Rights Acts in the U.S., or in 1975, when the Vietnamese people defeated the U.S. invasion, the air would be filled with hope. Third World peoples inside and outside the U.S. would be pushing an international antiracist agenda against the main enemy, U.S. imperialism—the political, economic, and military system of monopoly capitalism that subjugates whole nations and peoples.

At that revolutionary time in history, the strategic linkage of antiracism, national liberation, self-determination, and socialist economic development gave the Third World its moral and political power.

In Durban today, that strategy is needed more than ever. In the post-Cold War era, as the world balance of power has shifted, the antiracist movement is weak, disorganized, and in some instances, recolonized. The U.S. throws its weight around more than ever, no longer challenged by the former Soviet Union and formerly anti-imperialist Peoples Republic of China. Many Third World governments are enthusiastic or subordinated participants in neoliberal schemes, and the U.S. civil rights establishment, representing the privileged and bourgeois classes, functions as an appendage of the Democratic Party. As we approach WCAR, the big questions are: Will the U.S. and the Group of Eight (G8) colonial powers allow any debate at all?[1] Who will stand up to them?

The U.S. government is threatening to withdraw funding and boycott the conference altogether, ostensibly in protest against conference resolutions condemning Israeli racism and apartheid policies towards the Palestinian people and demands by Africans, U.S. Blacks, and peoples of the African Diaspora for reparations for the centuries of the U.S. and European Trans-Atlantic Slave Trade.

The US does not want the conference to take place.
They also want to cut funding for Blacks,

1. The Group of Eight Nations (G8)—which originally formed out of a meeting of the world's six largest economies in 1975—is composed of the United States, England, France, Germany, Canada, Italy, Japan and Russia. The G7 (the grouping before the addition of Russia in 1997) continues to meet separately on issues of global economic policy and is still the name used for the world's most economically dominant nations.

As 10,000 delegates prepare for the Non-Governmental Organization (NGO) forum (August 27-September 1) and the official United Nations governmental conference (August 31-September 7), many liberals in the U.S. are begging the Bush Administration to send a delegation. But whether the U.S. sends a "high level" delegation (with Colin Powell, Condoleezza Rice or John Ashcroft), or no delegation at all, its objectives are the same—the U.S. will try to undermine, suppress, and prevent the success of the conference and the rebuilding of a worldwide movement against racism. This is no time for Democrats and their liberal apologists to take cheap shots against Bush, for were Bill Clinton or Al Gore in power, their objectives, if not their methods, would be the same.

Remember, it was Clinton who destroyed "welfare as we know it" and permitted a national rampage against Black and Latina women and children. It was Clinton who signed the Effective Death Penalty Act that violated centuries of habeas corpus rights and made the imposition of the racist death penalty more "effective."[2] And it was House Democrats, including most members of the Congressional Black Caucus, who just passed House Resolution 212 that urged the U.S. to attend the WCAR, but which goes out of its way to oppose any discussion of Israeli racism or U.S. reparations to Black people. Instead, the House resolution urges U.S. governmental delegates to "mitigate, rather than aggravate, racial, ethnic, and regional tensions" by only discussing racism in general, "without reference to specific regions, countries, or present day conflicts"—the identical view of the Bush Administration.

Mann says Clinton would have done the same as Bush in regards to racism.

2. The Antiterrorism and Effective Death Penalty Act of 1996.

Whether under Republican or Democratic tactical leadership, the strategy of U.S. imperialism is to rule the world. In a society in which big business is king, U.S. led monopoly capitalism relies on profits and superprofits made possible by super-exploitation of human labor and nature in the Third World. It achieves these objectives by "integrating" Third World nations into an international economy structurally dominated by the International Monetary Fund, World Bank and World Trade Organization, which in turn, are controlled by the U.S.[3]

Under this totalitarian capitalist system, Third World nations are systematically underdeveloped through a global network that destroys their local industries, obliterates protective tariffs, penetrates their local markets, privatizes their national and natural resources, and impounds cash crops to feed Western banks. As Christian charities get rich exploiting pictures of emaciated Third World children, they used God to cover up the sinful

---

3. The IMF (International Monetary Fund) and the World Bank were both created at the Bretton Woods Conference in 1944 to help shape the post World War II international capitalist economy. The IMF and World Bank work in conjunction to restructure the economies of the Global South through the implementation of structural adjustment programs (SAPs), as a condition of loans made to developing nations. Often, SAPs take the form of austerity measures, including cuts in government spending on public services in favor of privatization, and requirements to open local markets to foreign trade and investment. Both operate under a decision making system whereby each nation's number of votes is determined by how much money it contributes to the institutions—allowing them to be dominated by the world's most wealthy countries, in particular the United States.

The WTO (World Trade Organization), formed by international treaty in 1995 with 144 member nations currently, is the body that develops and enforces laws of global free trade, which supercede the laws of nation states. The so-called QUAD countries (the U.S., Japan, Canada and the European Union) wield disproportionate power in decision making within the WTO. The WTO was established by Uruguay Round Negotiations (1984-94); its precursor was the General Agreements on Tariffs and Trade (GATT), which was also established at the Bretton Woods Conference.

Third world countries are in debt and thus are Controlled by US imperialism.

connection between Third World poverty and First World wealth, between structural racism and U.S. imperialism. Today, nations of the Third World are subordinated to the needs of the world's superpower; they are choking with debt repayments, their environment and ecosystems raped and pillaged, their people literally starving to death. The U.S., as the world's policeman, forcibly precludes the option for a social democratic, much less socialist, economy in any country in the world.

At the Durban conference, we can expect the U.S. and the European governments to try to decontextualize racism, to restrict its discussion to concerns about isolated acts of seemingly irrational and individual cruelty. By contrast, Left forces will try to draw the explosive and revolutionary connection between antiracism and anti-imperialism. The following assessments guide my expectations.

Organized forces from the U.S. and Africa are demanding reparations from the European and U.S. perpetrators of the Trans-Atlantic Slave Trade. In 1965, Malcolm X proposed that Black people bring their demands as a colonized people to the United Nations. In recent years, in the U.S., the Reparations Movement has been given focus by Randall Robinson's book, *The Debt: What America Owes to Blacks*, and a growing number of Black organizations that have made reparations their central focus.

The World Conference Against Racism will be marked by an important world confrontation on reparations, with the NGOs and many African governments proposing strong language for the final conference document, while the United States is leading the charge to prevent any discussions on the subject whatsoever. This already shows the value of the UN—as

Malcolm X understood—as an international forum; the U.S. will be forced to either defend its position or walk out, in either case a victory for the antiracist forces.

International condemnation of U.S. racist practices grows. Amnesty International's recent report, *Racism and the Administration of Justice*, published in preparation for WCAR, reports that "Black and ethnic minorities" constitute 60 percent of the 1.7 million people currently in jail in the U.S.[4] The racist character of the death penalty is demonstrated by cruel and unusual statistics: in Pennsylvania Blacks are 800 percent more likely to be executed than whites, in Georgia, 1100 percent. The war on drugs also reeks of racism; Blacks and Latinos constitute 63 percent, and whites 37 percent, of all drug offenders sent to state prison.

The UN Committee on the Elimination of Racial Discrimination noted that in the U.S. "members of minorities, (especially Blacks and Hispanics) may be disproportionately subject to adverse treatment throughout the criminal justice process."[5] These are seemingly meek words but courageous in terms of UN parlance.

Durban represents an international arena in which to help revitalize the U.S. antiracist movement. The Black Radical Congress, progressive Black legislators like Cynthia McKinney from Georgia and John Conyers from Michigan, grassroots groups

---

4. Amnesty International, *Racism and the Administration of Justice* (London: Amnesty International Publications, 2001), 22.

5. United Nations press release, "Committee on Elimination of Racial Discrimination Adopts Conclusions on Report of the United States," CERD 59th Session, 13 August 2001.

like the L.A. Bus Riders Union, the Center for Third World Organizing, and several key women of color organizations represent important pieces of the puzzle that make for a broad antiracist united front in the U.S. They are going to Durban in search of international allies. The questions remain: Can we build a functional and effective united front? Can we coalesce an opposition to U.S. governmental defiance? Can we find concrete ways to offer material support to Third World movements against racism and imperialism?

A growing South African resistance can shape the conference and the antiracist movement. South Africans are seeking allies as well. The Durban Social Forum, a new coalition of grassroots groups in South Africa, is planning demonstrations at the Conference to highlight the growing poverty and mass suffering in the post-Apartheid period. The Congress of South African Trade Unions (COSATU) is proposing "the mother of all strikes, a general strike" if the South African government does not abandon its neoliberal policies, which include the privatization of water and mass evictions from housing and land. How will those demonstrations, timed to pressure the South African government in the midst of an international conference in Durban, impact the actual deliberations and alliances at WCAR? What can the U.S. antiracist Left learn from the advanced theory and practice of the continuing South African revolution?

With these initial assessments, I go to South Africa with many questions. What is the strategy of the South African Communist Party and COSATU to challenge privatization and neoliberalism, the new face of international racism? Is there any form of organized Third World caucus or movement or tendency that is willing to challenge the U.S. at WCAR? And is it strong enough to force the discussion of Palestinian self-determination and Black and African reparations onto the front pages of the public debate? Is there a true left wing of the NGOs, or are most of them integrated into their own nation-states and world capitalism? Can the left, antiracist U.S. forces work in any coordinated fashion and toward what ends? Will the demonstrations by South Africans challenge the entire conference and create a new political reality on the streets? What roles will the People's Republic of China and Cuba play?

I go on this journey in two roles, with two goals. As a correspondent, I will find every way possible to give more voice to the voiceless, through my own *Dispatches From Durban*, distributed by the Labor/Community Strategy Center in Los Angeles, the *Black Radical Congress News*, and the South African Independent Media Center. As an organizer, I will try to demonstrate that there are Jews in the U.S. who care deeply about Palestinian rights, whites in the U.S. who want to challenge the racist policies of our government, Leftists who are committed to drawing constructive lessons from this historic event—as part of a strategy to help coalesce the left, anti-imperialist forces against racism.

I will keep you posted.

2

August 30, 2001
DURBAN

The COSATU General Strike and the Treachery of the International Marketplace

South Africans have raised marching for freedom to an art form. Today 100 delegates from the World Conference Against Racism (WCAR) NGO Forum, myself included, responded to a call by the Congress of South African Trade Unions (COSATU) to join the Durban march against privatization of public services. This was part of a two-day general strike, "the mother of all strikes" COSATU had hoped for, to challenge the neoliberal direction of the African National Congress (ANC) government, led by President Thabo Mbeki. Singing and dancing in a combined cultural, political, military event, we marched for four hours. Didn't know Zulu chants? No problem, they taught us.

In the second day of the strike, some 40,000 people filled the streets of Durban with wave upon wave of union contingents. This was not a trade union rally for a better contract; it was a nationwide political strike by Black working class and poor people for the future of their country. The call to strike? "We did not fight for liberation so that we could sell everything we won to the highest bidder!"

As the World Conference Against Racism NGO Forum prepares for the formal UN governmental agenda, the United States continues its political interference, attempting to dominate the UN agenda even as it threatens to not participate. The U.S. uses its visible and invisible hand to shape all world events.

But for the moment, my attention is fixed on the struggle of the host country, South Africa, to extend its revolution. During the last decades of the anti-Apartheid movement, most of the main revolutionary forces agreed there would be a two-stage revolution—the first, a democratic national liberation struggle to get rid of barbaric, fascist Apartheid; the second, to move South Africa toward a non-capitalist, pro-socialist form of economic and political development.[1]

---

1. This is distinct from a one-stage revolution which would have struggled to leap from Apartheid to socialism. Significantly, the first stage was completed with the 1994 democratic elections and drafting of the new Constitution of the Republic of South Africa, which guaranteed protection of property rights as well as reconciliation of racial antagonisms. While there are those who believe this settlement was too fundamental a compromise, the focus of the current struggle is not over the terms of the negotiations but rather what many see as the ANC's rapid abandonment of its earlier left social democratic strategy to constrain capital and its more recent adoption of a neoliberal one to unleash the free market. Today's march focused on opposition to privatization, a tool of neoliberalism not mandated by the new constitution's protections but pushed by those forces that want to accelerate South Africa's integration into the international economy.

But how do you get there? What does it really look like? This complex and open struggle over South Africa's post-Apartheid future is shaping the international debate over racism, national oppression and national liberation, and the World Conference Against Racism, as well as impacting the consciousness of the WCAR delegates.

The COSATU-led two-day general strike on the eve of WCAR is the focus of an increasingly public struggle. As we got off the plane in Durban, the blaring headlines in the South African *Sunday Times* declared "'COSATU leaders are liars'—Mbeki." In another headline, COSATU charged "distortions, half-truths, and character assassinations," in response to a statement released by government ministers accusing COSATU of trying to sabotage the World Conference Against Racism.

This is not a morality play, but a strategy play with implications for the entire world. The immediate subject of the debate? The strike is demanding that the government stop the sale of state assets while a new privatization policy is worked out. The *Sunday Times* quoted Thabo Mbeki, who once was an important figure on the world communist Left:

> One of the lies they [COSATU] tell us is that our government has betrayed policies agreed upon by the broad democratic movement with regard to the issue of restructuring state assets, thus, they argue that because of this we have betrayed the objectives of a better life for all.

Mbeki accused the COSATU leaders of using its members "as cannon fodder in an intensive effort aimed at defeating their own liberation movement."[2]

---

2. Simone Zwane, Ranjeni Munusamy, Sechaba Ka'Nkosi and Mondli Makhanya, "COSATU leaders are liars—Mbeki," *Sunday Times*, 26 August 2001.

In response, the National Union of Mineworkers (a member of COSATU) General Secretary Gwede Mantashe said the strike would send a message to the governing African National Congress that "a mandate to govern is not a blank cheque." Leading 300,000 mineworkers across the nation into the strike, he charged,

> ...we are fast approaching a stage in our movement where there are those who want to centralize power in order to kill off organizational structures. It is to the advantage of those in power to have weak structures. They are very nervous. A clear picture is emerging of an ANC that was elected by the left working class and is governing for the right-wing middle class.[3]

The current struggle is not over "privatization in general"; all the parties of the united front Tripartite Alliance—between the ANC, COSATU and the South African Communist Party (SACP)—have agreed to the privatization of public resources to some extent.[4] Many COSATU and SACP rank-and-file, however, angrily charge that no such choice was put in front of them by their own leadership, let alone by the Mbeki ANC government. Perhaps because of that rank-and-file pressure, the COSATU and SACP leadership are now arguing that the process has gone too far.

The government shifted from the social democratic Reconstruction and Development Programme (RDP) that emphasized

---

3. "COSATU leaders are liars—Mbeki," *Sunday Times,* 26 August 2001.

4. The Tripartite Alliance is the most commonly used name for the Revolutionary Alliance formalized in the early 1990s between the ANC, COSATU and the South African Communist Party (SACP), which grew out of the earlier Congress Alliance of the 1950s.

expanding the public sector to the neoliberal Growth, Employment And Redistribution (GEAR) program that focuses on
expanding the private sector.[5] As a result, private capital is
still fleeing the country while basic services—food, water, energy, housing—are being denied. The poor cannot afford to
make any payments and free public resources are urgently
needed. (This debate—over whether water, food, and medicine are human rights or are commodities to be sold in the
market—is shaping the entire struggle about Third World development across the globe.)

Mbeki's argument is that privatization is a tactic to attract
and retain urgently needed domestic and foreign capital—either
as an inducement or as a necessary concession. In that context,
Mbeki's rhetorical jibe at COSATU as those who "claim easy
victories over the colonial and Apartheid legacy" essentially argues that the ANC is in governance now and those who think
that it is so easy should try it themselves.

The basis for this argument is that there are white racists
throughout the country including still-armed white paramilitary

---

5. When the African National Congress first came to power in 1994, many
called its Reconstruction and Development Program (RDP) a left social
democratic program. The ANC understood it was trying to govern a capitalist
economy but during this period focused on the expansion of the public sector, the
use of state funds to build up social programs, and governmental regulation and
intervention in the economy, including measures to increase taxes on South African
capitalists' profits in order to increase the financial base of the government. In 1996,
the ANC leadership, led by then Executive Deputy President Thabo Mbeki,
introduced GEAR (Growth Employment And Redistribution) which explicitly accepts
free market forces as the key to rebuilding South Africa's economy and accepts the
primacy of international financial markets. For a comprehensive critique of GEAR
and the broader neoliberal agenda for South Africa, see Patrick Bond, *Elite
Transition* (London: Pluto Press, 2000).

groups and capitalists holding key economic assets; warfare between some indigenous peoples and nations of Africa is still a danger; and the ANC is compelled to find ways to placate some conservative forces among the Zulu people represented by the Inkatha Freedom Party and not alienate them further from the ANC government. Some in the ANC argue that since capital is fleeing South Africa and the new government needs national and foreign investment, privatization opens up new avenues for capital investment, reduces state expenditures, and creates new opportunities for taxation.

Without possible support for independence from a no-longer-existing Soviet Union, the Mbeki tendency, the governing tendency in the ANC, argues that the main method by which to consolidate the anti-Apartheid revolution is to strengthen the power of the government and to successfully integrate South Africa into the international economy.[6]

---

6. In this discussion, I am focusing on the debate about privatization, because that is the issue that COSATU has framed. But in my many discussions with South African and international activists, organizers, and intellectuals, there is another important debate unfolding about Black power versus "non-racialism" and how those objectives should be addressed. This debate spans disagreements about the wisdom and specific tactics about the Truth and Reconciliation Commission, but also about the challenge of what to do about the post-Apartheid concentration of private wealth in white hands. As part of the negotiated settlement that the anti-Apartheid forces entered into with the white Apartheid government, the parties agreed, as I understand it, that there would be strong protection of property rights and that any transfer of private land would be based on the market concept of "willing buyer, willing seller." But at an important series of debates that took place at the University of South Africa, Durban, Ibo Mandaza, a Zimbabwean Marxist from *Southern Africa Review of Political Economy,* warned the South African ANC leaders, including SACP General Secretary Blade Nzimande; "If you do not pass laws and policies that allow the government to

In contrast, the left COSATU leadership argues that while aware of these contradictions, far too many concessions are being made to international capital and to a burgeoning Black bourgeoisie. Some COSATU and SACP members argue that the state faces a challenge—if it does not seize or commandeer or purchase at fair prices the resources of whites, if it does not tax capital and risk capital flight, it may find itself with little state or private capital at all and risk a lifetime of indebtedness to the G8 and its many structures of economic and social domination, including the WTO, IMF, World Bank.

For now, COSATU is beginning with the demand that the government stop privatizing, and it is calling for top-level negotiations with the government about the specific policies and consequences that will be required to protect public assets.

The growing political conflict between COSATU and the ANC government should not be interpreted as a split. At this

---

forcibly take land from whites under eminent domain, and redistribute it to the Black poor, and if you do not do it now, you will face the problem in ten or twenty years as we do, and it will tear the country apart." "In Zimbabwe today," the speaker continued, "the government, under President Robert Mugabe, is instituting a limited policy of land confiscation from white farmers, as the Black farmers do not have enough land to grow enough crops to feed their families, let alone export. And yet, the international media is so racist, and so protective of white property, that the picture of a white farmer in handcuffs, escorted away from 'his' land by Black police, was so offensive to the whites in England they talked about an invasion of our country, while the picture of a Black man with his head cut off by racists would not evoke a similar outrage. You in South Africa have a dilemma: a market economy cannot serve the poor and a 'non-racial' state that does not have specific programs to redistribute land on a racial basis to the Black poor will be built on an unstable foundation." That debate, at times implicit and at times explicit in the landless movement, is another structural challenge in the post-Apartheid struggle for reconstruction.

point these are still tactical contradictions between strategic allies. The complex Tripartite Alliance between the ANC, COSATU and the SACP is defined as a "strategic partnership." To understand the complexity, it helps to know that these are not simply three separate coalition partners:

☐ All COSATU and SACP members are in the ANC, or at least vote for the ANC at election time. Some key COSATU and SACP leaders as well as many middle level officials hold elected and appointed office in the ANC government, some of whom hold top ministerial level positions in the national government.

☐ Many COSATU leaders and members are also members of the SACP.

☐ Several key ministers in the ANC government, including some who have supported the GEAR program and the present focus on privatization, are members of both SACP and COSATU. And some of them have taken a very hard line against the Left (including the leaders of their own organizations) in "defense" of the government's policies.

At the same time, it is widely agreed that COSATU and the SACP leadership have been losing some credibility with the rank-and-file members and the overall working class as the growing poverty, homelessness, and deterioration of social services is reaching national crisis proportions.

Something bold had to be done to impact government policy. In this context, the two-day general strike is a major show of force by the majority of the COSATU leadership to establish its own power, its own independence in the formal Alliance united front. And similar to anti-globalization and antiracist groups in the U.S. that used the Democratic or Republican national conventions as international media arenas to popularize their demands, COSATU is taking advantage of Mbeki's tactical vulnerability during the World Conference Against Racism.

At a time when Mbeki wants to showcase South Africa as a center for world tourism and to use tourism as a source of urgently needed foreign exchange funds, a two-day general strike is the last thing he wanted. This contributed to the greater leverage and impact of the march, but also to the bitterness of the exchanges between its leaders and the South African government.

While there are some who talk as if the ANC is a petit-bourgeois party, it is in fact a multi-class party whose membership is overwhelmingly Black working class. Whether the Mbeki leadership serves the interests of the Black working class is another question. The widespread sense of betrayal by the government at the grassroots is reflected in charges that the government broke its promises on the redistribution of land and the provision of housing, and in anger at the Truth and Reconciliation process. A hotel employee I interviewed had a typical response:

> Many of us lost our fathers and mothers, lost our livelihood during Apartheid, and yet all the white people had to do was to say they were sorry and admit their guilt and they got to keep their jobs, their pensions, their everything, and we still have nothing except an apology. We thought we would be compensated by the government, and instead, now they are taking away our government services.[7]

---

7. Interview with the author, 28 August, 2001

Everybody I have talked to says that the fight over privatization is a genuine mass struggle from below. While the official COSATU line is "moratorium" until they "reclarify" what privatization means, the masses of marching workers are saying, "Let us clarify it for you. Hands off the parks, hands off the schools, hands off hospitals, telecommunications, energy and water. Basic needs cannot be privatized."

Watching thousands of workers in the streets, I am moved by the motion of the masses and by the fact that socialism is a mass question here. Almost every union has a slogan about socialism on their banners that spread across the street. "Fight for national liberation and socialism!" The line put out most clearly was, "We can't keep talking about socialism if we give away the building blocks of socialism: all the basic services needed for the survival of the working class, controlled by the working class through the government." Whether or not they can hold on to these building blocks remains to be seen.

As the strikers marched today through Durban, the dynamic relationship between the liberation movement and the masses was evident. It was hard to know where the contingents of marchers ended and where the supporters on the street began—as would be bystanders often jumped into line, marched with us for a few miles, and then peeled off, replaced by another street battalion. Some of the chanters were pros, well-known performance artists. This is public art, public entertainment. There could have been awards for best street moves, best long-distance energy, best original chant—as the march continued into its third hour, it generated a rhythm of its own, in which we were simultaneously tired and energized—the march could have gone on for another day if it had to. After four hours of marching, we convened on the steps of Durban's city hall. Speaker after speaker denounced privatization, with call and response: "Amandla, Ngawethu!" meaning "the power is ours." And "Vivas" for everyone: "Viva COSATU, Viva!" "Viva SACP, Viva!" "Long live socialism, Long live!"

One highlight of the rally was a solidarity speech by Black Radical Congress member Ashaki Binta from Atlanta, Georgia who spoke on behalf of the Charleston Five. These were dock workers, four Black and one white, from Local 1422 of the International Longshoremen's Association in Charleston, South Carolina who were arrested for militant demonstrations trying to stop non-union scabs from breaking their union. They were facing serious jail time if convicted by a racist, union-hating, "right to work" attorney general.[8]

But Binta did not come to simply generate support for one labor struggle from another; hers was a strategy to build international support among Black workers in particular all over the world. Binta addressed the COSATU workers: "I come to you as an African sister who was kidnapped and separated from you centuries ago. Do you recognize me?" After she spoke, a COSATU leader embraced her and put his face right next to hers. Speaking to the crowd he said, "Is this not my sister, my kidnapped sister, am I not her brother?" and the crowd roared in pain but also in exaltation: Despite the bitter struggle against privatization, these were Black workers who had slain the dragon of Apartheid.

---

8. On November 8, 2001, after a successful campaign led by labor and the Black community, the charges were dropped.

The inspiring speeches went on and on, but at a certain point in the program the speakers began to lose connection with the masses. As speech after speech denounced privatization, one worker turned to another and said, "So where is all this going? What is the plan?" The speakers from COSATU and SACP were offering no clear tactical guidance as to how the demonstration fit into a larger campaign strategy. How would the general strike lead to negotiations with the government? What were the main tactical objectives of those negotiations? Eventually, the crowd began to disperse. The general strike and the mass march had not in fact shut industry or the country down, but it was effective as a militant vote of no confidence in ANC government policy. Yet, how would COSATU and the SACP impact the overall strategic partnership with the ANC and the Mbeki government? How does a movement reverse privatization or at least stop it in its tracks?

Contrary to Mbeki's fear that the general strike would embarrass the host nation, the openness of this struggle, before an international audience, brings credit to South Africa. It highlights the pressure imposed on national liberation movements, especially when they succeed, to submit to the treachery of the international marketplace. The South African revolution emancipated its people from colonial and white minority domination. Yet, the exploitation of nations that is the very foundation of imperialism still sets the stage for South Africa's political struggle over the terms of its integration into the global economy.

In my two weeks in Durban, I have witnessed two major demonstrations by South Africans against their government—the COSATU general strike, and another mass protest by the Durban Social Forum, a broad coalition of groups led by the landless, demanding land, water, jobs, housing, and an end to neoliberal economic and social policies. And yet in the streets of Durban, there is very little protest directly against the United States—the primary force behind the very structural adjustments and distortions of South Africa society and the strongest backer of white South African capital in the world.

So, as the South Africans march against their government, we will march against the U.S. While of course it will require an international movement, those of us in the United States—antiracists, anti-imperialists, human rights advocates, and all those who care about the future of democracy and viable national liberation in the Global South—must fight the abuses of our own government and the system that produces them. As the South Africans continue to struggle over the best direction for their revolution, we who are participating in the UN World Conference Against Racism can find no better illustration of—and opportunity to protest—the omnipresence of the United States.

I will keep you posted.

- Strike against gov't (S.African)
- demands for land, water, jobs, housing and an end to neoliberal economic and social policies.

South African Workers Protest Against Privatization: Amy Goodman Interviews Mahlengi Bengu & Eric Mann

September 3, 2001
DURBAN

Transcript:

Amy Goodman reporting from Durban, South Africa at the World Conference Against Racism

Segment Story: **SOUTH AFRICAN WORKERS PROTEST AGAINST PRIVATIZATION**

Guests:

- ☐ Mahlengi Bengu, Chief Education Officer, COSATU (Congress of South African Trade Unions).

- ☐ Eric Mann, a member of the Planning Committee of the L.A. Bus Riders Union and the director of the Labor/Community Strategy Center, and is in Durban for the conference.

Introduction

In what is believed to be the biggest protest since the end of white rule in 1994, millions of South African workers last week participated in a two-day general strike against the privatization of public services.

The strike, called by the Congress of South African Trade Unions, or COSATU, has shaken the ruling so-called Tripartite Alliance between the dominant African National Congress (ANC), the South African Communist Party (SACP), and COSATU.

Tensions between the three mounted after the ANC took power with the first multiracial, democratic elections in 1994. According to critics, the ANC gave away too much to multinational corporations, in an attempt to lure international investors. Now, some say the ANC has sold out, and is just towing the neoliberal line.

Today, on Labor Day, we're joined by COSATU's Chief Education Officer, as well as Los Angeles Bus Riders Union member Eric Mann, who is in Durban for the conference and marched with the COSATU workers last week.

Interview with Mahlengi Bengu

Amy Goodman: Can you talk about the protest of last Friday? Tell us about this two-day strike and why you chose to do it exactly at the time of the World Conference Against Racism taking place in Durban.

Mahlengi Bengu: What is important to spell out from the outset is that COSATU for a very long time, alongside other working class formations in South Africa, has been engaged in government and in other elements of the state regarding the best way in which we need to build the capacity of the state. And obviously, it has been argued that one of the best ways of doing so is to manage properly the assets that are owned by the state, which is what the strike was about. And these discussions have been taking place for a very long time, actually for years, about a framework within which the restructuring of the state-owned enterprises as part and parcel of the democratization and deracialization of South Africa society have to be managed.

So it wasn't just a one-time decision to hold the strike during the proceedings of the World Conference Against Racism. There are key issues around which government and labor have not found one another and we don't see this as simply an economic strike. It is also about defending the rights of the South African majority who struggled for many years so they have access to water, electricity, food, and bread in their stomachs. So it's not just about narrow short-term questions. Well, of course we will do that as trade unions, but this time around it is a strike around which we want to mobilize the entirety of South African society and the other global forces so that we intensify struggles against privatization wherever it takes place, not only in South Africa.

Amy Goodman: Now the government of South Africa beseeched COSATU not to have this strike at the time of the conference. It just finished up before the conference began. Why did COSATU stand firm on the date?

Mahlengi Bengu: Well, I think our view—that of the federation, which is supported and mandated by the two million members that we have, as well as the broader support base that COSATU enjoys in South African society—is that we had to stand firm. Had to stand firm because we know that even though we have achieved formal political democracy, since 1994 and, mark my words, when I use the word formal political democracy, it simply means that without transforming the economy, building a strong, developmental and democratic state. Without that, formal political democracy remains hollow. So we've got to intensify the struggle. We struggled for an ANC-led government; we will continue to support it. But we will defend workers in the entire working class whenever we see that their interests are being undermined. And we've certainly seen that government policy on privatization—which they call the restructuring of state-owned enterprises—rolls back a number of struggles that workers of this country have led.

Amy Goodman: We are talking to Mahlengi Bengu, Chief Education Officer for COSATU, the Congress of South Africa Trade Unions, live in Durban, South Africa where the UN World Conference Against Racism is taking place.

Mahlengi Bengu, COSATU has agreed to limited privatization in the past. Can you talk about that?—as has the South African Communist Party.

Mahlengi Bengu: Yes, I think that it is very important to explain the point. There are what are known as state-owned enterprises, or public enterprises as they normally call them in South Africa. That includes organizations of companies such as Transnet, which is responsible for rail and transport, Fornet which is responsible for rail, Portnet which is responsible for harbors, Escom responsible for electricity, Telecom, responsible for telecommunications. These are just examples, of very huge state-owned enterprises that command a lot of the capital that could be best used to support development. Now, we also have other state owned enterprises, such as Avensura which is responsible for tourism, holidays, managing holiday resorts, etc.

Now, obviously, COSATU's fixation is really with the kinds of state-owned enterprises which provide the services that are really basic for human survival and sustainable livelihood. And the kinds of state-owned enterprises that will contribute through ensuring that we deliver clean water to people. We deliver sanitation, we deliver food, and we think those are very basic. We deliver electricity to a majority of rural people who have not had electricity for a very long time. And we are saying that those kind of enterprises, under no circumstances should they be privatized, because once they are privatized the interests of private enterprise is different from what should be the interests of an emerging national democratic state, which is what we are still fighting for. We have not achieved that as yet.

That is different from Avensura, which may have auxiliary services, that it manages. And we have seen that in the interests of managing state-owned enterprises, restructuring is in order. Restructuring is in order because the upper state has no interest in providing services, and basic services to people, especially to the Black majority. Now we are having to expand the mandate of the state-owned enterprises, so that they are able to cater to the historically oppressed Black majority. There is a need for some form of restructuring so that they are efficient and they are able to work effectively.

Now that is really where we are. We are not hung up on an ideological construction of privatization which is usually interpreted to mean that nothing can ever be thrown to the private sector. The private sector can handle administration of some of those holiday resorts, in our view. However, we think that you cannot hand over management of the delivery of electricity to the majority of South Africans. And I think that those two services, tourism and water supply delivery, are qualitatively different from the point of view of a country that has been ravished by a state of poverty and inequality. For the majority of us, a tourist facility is very luxurious. And we think that we need to start there. We can have a discussion later on down the line about how we manage our tourism. Obviously we know it is an important income generator. Obviously I'm just picking up on one example.

We are not supporting privatization, but we are saying that what is known as non-core assets could be privatized, could be commercialized. So, that is really where we stand. Let me say that with water, electricity and Telecom for instance, the installation of telephones, those should not be left to the private sector because the private sector in South Africa, and globally, has proved that they are not interested in making a dent against or contributing to a fight against poverty and inequality. So we've been very consistent on that line. We mobilized workers to vote for the ANC on the basis of basic service delivery that is going to be driven and led by the state that is strong, that continues to build its capacity so that it is able to efficiently deliver basic services to our people.

Amy Goodman: What role does the World Bank and the IMF play in these issues of privatization?

Mahlengi Bengu: Well, as you know South Africa is presently assuming front and center stage within the global community, but more particularly within the financial institutions that you just referred to. And we are saying that the policies that we have committed ourselves to politically—through the manifestos, and as you go and vote as South Africans, and as a new government—

are largely inconsistent with the policies within the WTO, within the IMF, and within the World Bank. And we are calling on our government to actually use its own influence within those structures to challenge what is taking place there. We know for instance that privatization is largely shaped and influenced by the neoliberal framework that South Africa, as a component of the UN system and a number of financial institutions, has not been able to challenge in the manner in which we would like to see that happening. But we know that, in fact, we can't just make calls. We've got to mobilize our workers, our members; we've got to mobilize workers in general, and other social formations in South Africa so that we can build a strong mass movement in this country that is able to consistently engage our own government and support our government when we think they are taking on a progressive path that not only benefits South Africa but benefits a majority of the world's working people.

Amy Goodman: Thank you, Mahlengi Bengu of COSATU the Congress of South African Trade Unions in Durban, South Africa.

Interview with Eric Mann

Amy Goodman: Eric Mann is here with Mahlengi Bengu. He marched in the COSATU strike. Eric Mann is a member of the Planning Committee of the Los Angeles Bus Riders Union and Director of the Labor/Community Strategy Center, in Durban for the Conference. He spent ten years as a United Auto Workers union assembly line worker in the U.S.

Eric, you were part of the COSATU march. I read one of the commentaries you put out, "The COSATU Strike and the Treachery of the International Marketplace." Can you talk about the connections between what is going on in South Africa and what you see in Los Angeles?

Eric Mann: On a very positive note, the Ninth Circuit District Court of the United States ruled just yesterday to *uphold* the Bus Riders Union civil rights case against the Metropolitan Transportation Authority! This is a tremendous victory for the civil rights movement in the U.S. against the Scalia court, a fortunate development to be happening while I am in Durban.

Marching with the workers in COSATU, one of the things I was thinking about was the tremendous pressure that they are under and how the debate gets framed as, "should Mbeki do this?" or "should COSATU do this?" And the United States is outside the debate, when in fact the United States' hands are all over this World Conference Against Racism. The United States, in my opinion, subverted the NGO conference and is in the process now of subverting the UN conference.

One of the things I was thinking is that if we developed a demand for reparations in the United States that dealt with the Trans-Atlantic Slave Trade it would delegitimize the U.S. government here in Africa and take pressure off the South African government so that they can have genuine self-determination. To ask what Mbeki should do inside the IMF and the World Bank assumes that South Africa is the equal of the U.S. in these international arenas when the U.S. threatens to withdraw capital, when the U.S. threatens to withdraw loans, when Mercedes threatens that if you go on strike, "we are going to pull the capital out of South Africa." I think that people in the United States should be focusing more on the U.S. government's policies than engaging in internal debates about what the South African working class should do.

It was pretty incredible to march with 40,000-50,000 workers in South Africa teaching us Zulu chants, teaching us dance steps, and seeing the way that the working class is received in this country; seeing posters that say "national liberation and socialism." And, if I could add, one of the things some of the COSATU members said was, "look, we don't have socialism now, but how can we move toward socialism if we give away the state assets?" It's not just a question of what is the best way to run the government. The Black working class has taken power in South Africa, and one of the things it has is state assets.

It is exciting to be here. Then you discuss the AFL-CIO in the U.S., by contrast, I am very sad about the narrowness of U.S. labor politics and very deeply moved by the broadness of COSATU's politics.

Amy Goodman: Eric Mann, in terms of your own struggle, the L.A. Bus Riders Union, can you talk about what is happening there as it relates to issues of privatization?

Eric Mann: Yes, in fact being here helps me understand our own issue better. The issue in Los Angeles is that the State, instead of privatizing itself, has become a vehicle for private capital. The MTA has moved three billion dollars in money to boondoggle rail projects to go out to the white suburbs and has bled the inner city bus system used by 400,000 overwhelmingly minority-nationality bus riders. This is a different form of privatization. Rather than taking capital outside of the State, it is using state capital to help construction companies, rail companies, Black and Latino bourgeois contractors. Essentially, it is diverting the surplus away from the working class towards the privileged classes. It is a very classic, in some ways, IMF development model of structural adjustment, and I think, in marching with the COSATU workers, that we have to use those expressions better in L.A. We say "fight transit racism"; I think we also have to say "fight structural adjustment," "fight the seizure of state assets," as COSATU is saying.

One other thing I have to say is that we need to get our dance steps better. We are pretty good in L.A., but I have learned a lot here that I want to bring back about a truly vibrant mass movement. I think people in communities of color inside the United States, whether it be in New York, Chicago, or Detroit, Atlanta should start using more explicit Third World terminology—not rhetorically but analytically—to explain that, in significant ways, our cities really are like Third World cities inside a First World country.

Amy Goodman: Well, this is Eric Mann from the Bus Riders Union and Mahlengi Bengu from COSATU, live in Durban, South Africa at the World Conference Against Racism.

September 4, 2001
DURBAN

U.S. Government Walkout Galvanizes U.S. NGO Delegation

Both sides came to Durban spoiling for a fight. The U.S. governmental delegation of the Bush administration, fresh from having stolen an election by denying Black votes, was threatening to walk out from the minute it learned about the World Conference Against Racism (WCAR). Most U.S. non-governmental organization (NGO) delegates had contempt for the U.S. governmental team. The militant radicals, Black nationalists, and antiracist organizers hated the whole two-party system, while even the more accomodationist Democrats were liberals who hated Bush with a passion. So the fight was on from the get go. The only question was what form it would take.

It was the eve of Labor Day in the U.S. and 400 U.S. delegates to the NGO Forum filed into the large lecture hall at UNISA (University of South Africa at Durban). We had come, ostensibly, to hear a report to the non-governmental organizations from the shell of the U.S. governmental delegation to WCAR.

As we entered the room, all hell broke loose. Rumors spread that the U.S. delegation had no intention to report to us. Wade Henderson, from the National Leadership Conference on Civil Rights, announced that last-minute negotiations with the U.S had broken down and that it was almost inevitable that the U.S. governmental delegation would make good on its threat to walk out of WCAR altogether.

Almost immediately, the 400 NGO delegates from the U.S. began to debate whether or not we should launch an immediate march and protest against the U.S. walkout in support of racism. About 200 of the delegates voted with their feet and left, some disagreeing with the protest tactic, others having strong political disagreements rooted in past political associations with other NGO delegates. That left 200 of us to transform the group into a viable ad hoc force to protest U.S. policies at the conference.

Many of the delegates did not know each other at all, many had political disagreements, and some had prior histories of unity or outright antagonism. Yet we worked successfully in a multiracial, majority-Black group led by Black women.

Within fifteen minutes we had formed an action coalition. In order to move effectively, we worked to clarify our political line. Earlier in the conference, more moderate U.S. NGO forces had focused primarily on the question of the absence of the U.S. delegation. "Where is the U.S.?" they had asked, expressing the view that if the U.S. did not attend, the conference would be compromised. Yet, by the end of a week of haggling over resolutions in the NGO Forum, there was now far greater unity of anger against the U.S. government for its presence.

The U.S. governmental delegation, along with other Western countries, had tried to intimidate NGO delegates into meaningless, toothless declarations against racism in general with no mention of specific countries or specific atrocities or, specific policies of redress and reparations. There was tremendous anger at the way the U.S. had approached the entire conference, beginning with its early use of threats as a way to bully the many other countries for whom the UN is a critical vehicle. Barbara Arnwine of the Lawyers Committee for Civil Rights commented,

> The U.S. withdrawal is the first principled thing that the U.S. has done. There is a profound conflict of interest in that the U.S. is the main source of world racism. How can it come and try to impose its will on a world conference *against* racism?

There was widespread agreement that the issue of U.S. reparations to Africa, Blacks in the U.S., and the peoples of the African Diaspora for the Trans-Atlantic Slave Trade had to be the main focus of our demands—a position the U.S. government had vehemently opposed. Yet, the U.S. delegation had also cloaked its walk-out in mock outrage over Palestinian demands for self-determination and the charges that the Israeli state itself was based on racist ideology and practice—Zionism as Apartheid. Thus the question was raised: How should we challenge the U.S., in particular, for its use of Israel as a foil to withdraw participation?

Several delegates argued that while they were in support of the Palestinian cause, they felt it was deflecting focus away from the demands for Black reparations. This led to a spirited and somewhat heated debate. Sandra Jaribu Hill, an attorney from Mississippi, argued that she believed the Palestinian issue was not a "diversion" but a central focus in the world struggle against racism and imperialism. She raised the question, "How can Blacks in the U.S. isolate themselves from such a front-line struggle, especially one that is under tremendous attack and in so much need of worldwide support?" Others expressed concern that there was even a tendency in the reparations movement to focus too much on Blacks within the U.S. and to downplay solidarity with the nations of Africa, the Caribbean, and Latin America.

As my first commentary expressed, one of my original objectives was to help demonstrate that there are Jews in the U.S. who care deeply about Palestinian rights and who are outraged at Israeli racism and conquest, as well as whites in the U.S. who want to challenge the racist policies of our government—as part of a strategy to help coalesce the left, anti-imperialist forces against racism. In the midst of the heated debate among the U.S. protestors, and the U.S. charges that it was walking out as a protest against "anti-Semitism," I made the following comments to our ad hoc group:

> As a Jew, I am very upset about the provocative role that the U.S. and Israel are playing at the conference in trying to make it seem like those of us who support Palestinian self-determination, or the return of all Israeli-occupied land, or even those who question the entire Israeli state from its inception are anti-Semitic.

They even call those of us who hate Israeli aggression 'self-hating Jews.' I am of course outraged by anti-Semitism, but my focus for redress is on the German holocaust and U.S. complicity with it, not the forcible confiscation of land from the Palestinians who were colonial subjects. Like many Jews who joined the civil rights movement and the Black liberation movement, I was moved into action by my experience of anti-Semitism from Christian whites, not Blacks, not Palestinians.

While, of course, there is anti-Semitism and even anti-Semites in all movements, including the Palestinian movement, the Palestinian movement itself is not anti-Semitic. It is a movement for national liberation. The Israelis want to leave the conference because they do not want to subject their policies to an international debate—53 years of occupation of Palestinian lands, the murder of Palestinian civilians in violation of the Nuremberg statutes, the denial of a viable homeland to the Palestinian people, and now the new tactic of targeted missile assassinations of Palestinian leaders.

In fact, the U.S. is an anti-Semitic country that does not give a damn about Jews or for that matter about Israel; rather, the U.S. government is using Israel as its stalking horse in the Middle East and at this conference. Moreover, the Israeli government and the political movement of Zionism, are not the same as Jews, do not speak for all Jews, but rather represent a specific political tendency among the Jews of the world. As we all must make choices in life, I stand with the Palestinians.

After further discussion and debate, more than 90 percent of the 200 remaining U.S. NGO delegates voted to prioritize the demands for reparations, Palestinian self-determination, and censure of Israeli racism and brutality. These were the demands we felt should be at the frontline of WCAR's agenda, and, by no accident, they were the key demands over which the U.S. chose to walk out.

Several people proposed that we attempt to seat ourselves as the "real" U.S. delegation, in the spirit of the Mississippi Freedom Democratic Party challenge of 1964. But others observed that in fact we had no legitimacy to represent U.S. NGOs, let alone any social movements in the U.S.; we had the right and obligation to protest, but to be careful about who we did and did not represent. Still, the idea in microcosm was important. What if, at some time in the future, a more unified U.S. antiracist movement was able to agree upon a united front of delegates representing important constituencies and movements in the U.S.? This discussion shed light on the present state of disunity and disorganization of the movement and challenged us to continue this work at home.

We agreed on a group of spokespeople that included Adjua Aiyetoro, Linda Roots, Thema Bryant, Juana-Majel Dixon, Youmna Chlala, Ai-Jen Poo and myself. It was time to stop talking and start marching. We took to the streets with the plan to converge in a rally in front of the Durban International Convention Center, several blocks away. Others joined us as we chanted,

"Stop U.S. Racism—All Over the World,"

"The People, United, Will Never Be Defeated."

Many Third World delegates, standing along the streets, cheered us onward—happy to see U.S. NGOs taking on the U.S. government. The militancy and politics of the demonstration attracted international media coverage as we had hoped, with

CNN running a feed that was seen throughout South Africa and at least as far as Los Angeles.

We reconvened the next morning for a rally targeting U.S. actions at the conference that took on a life of its own. We had a movement of 200 spokespeople, talking into microphones and cameras. Indigenous people took center stage. Meanwhile that morning, the U.S governmental delegation officially withdrew from the conference as expected, allegedly in protest against "anti-Israeli" statements.

Some in the bourgeois press claimed that the Palestinians and Arabs had "hijacked" the conference by not compromising with the "reasonable" European and Israeli powers. Others commented that the U.S. walkout had fatally damaged the chance for a "unity of action" on world racism, essentially sinking all hopes for a successful outcome for the conference. One more thoughtful reporter at the *South African Mail & Guardian* did tell it like it is, that in fact the U.S. used the struggle over Israeli policy as a pretext to leave the conference because it feared the debate about the Trans-Atlantic Slave Trade, the culpability of the U.S. and Europe in "crimes against humanity," and the inevitable and logical programmatic response of massive reparations to the nations of Africa and Black people in the Diaspora, including inside the U.S.

Our press rally represented only one tendency within the broader U.S. NGO arena—this tendency was a united front, I would say, between the Black nationalist Left in its various ideological reflections, the antiracist, anti-imperialist, pro-socialist Left (in this instance, also majority Black), and the environmental justice groups in the U.S. rooted in low-income communities of color.

Black nat'l Left
and
pro-socialist Left   vs.   US.

Even with the tremendous lack of unity in the U.S. Left in general, this group, despite many differences of philosophy and strategy, managed to develop unity of action, agree upon spokespeople, and pull off a spontaneous but effective rally within hours. In a small but significant way, the U.S. NGO delegates offered a counter-hegemonic analysis, conveying successfully to people in the U.S. and in the UN conference itself that there is another voice in the United States. In fact, for a day and a half there was widespread outrage among all the U.S. NGO delegates.

By noon the anger and energy had dissipated, and we had to reintegrate ourselves into the daily technicalities of the UN conference or find other things to do. I chose to attend two workshops of more than 500 people each. One addressed the problems of indigenous women, with ten impressive speakers each expressing outrage and first-hand organizing stories of resistance by the more than 400 million indigenous peoples throughout the world—from Hawaii, to Colombia, to Nigeria, to Sudan. Their main demand was that the United Nations recognize the independent political and social status and rights of indigenous peoples, even if that means challenging the power of the nation-states that are subordinating Indigenous peoples' rights.

The second mass workshop was on reparations, led by African scholars and activists, focusing in detail on the Trans-Atlantic Slave Trade. In this workshop the primary emphasis was on the importance of popularizing detailed historical documentation of the specificity of the slave trade, in all its painful, horrible details, in order to set the moral, intellectual, political, and legal foundation for the most profound and structural demands against European nations and the United States.

The U.S. walkout and the U.S. NGO protest could turn out to be an important historical event or simply an inconsequential blip on the screen of history. In terms of my sense of historical optimism, the event's most important possibilities reside in its model for future international resistance, and the incremental steps toward rebuilding a U.S. antiracist Left.

Harking back to the Mississippi Freedom Democratic Party (MFDP) challenge of 1964: a predominantly Black MFDP challenged the lily-white Mississippi party and demanded to be seated—causing a massive civil war within the Democratic party and the Lyndon Johnson election team, and generating one of the pivotal events of the civil rights movement at the time. Many U.S. NGO delegates, showing our age by that reference, referred back to a time when people all over the country had worked together on the MFDP fight, the many Marches on Washington against the war, the Woolworth's boycott, the Selma March, and the New Haven Black Panther trials. Today, the facile slogan, "Think globally, act locally" covers up the absence of a national and international movement. There is no way to defeat or even curtail transnational capitalism at the local level alone. It is only through building local, city-wide and regional bases that left forces can reach out to broader arenas of action. Building an international movement from a solid local base makes sense, but doing local work in isolation is fundamentally a dead-end.

In Durban, many forces in the U.S. antiracist movement worked together to protest the U.S walkout. Direct action against a common enemy is liberating, but also instructive. The way people speak at meetings or handle differences and conflicts can reflect either too much unity or too much struggle in the united front. Sometimes you don't agree with somebody at a meeting but you watch them in a march or protest or dealing with the police and change your opinion, often for the better. For example, I went to Durban as the only representative from my organization—the Labor/Community Strategy Center in Los Angeles—but made many new allies there, and came back with story after story of people I met at Durban with whom I want to work in the future.

As I write this, I am already planning to go to the UN World Summit on Sustainable Development (WSSD) in Johannesburg in August of 2002, as part of a six-person Strategy Center delegation. I am convinced that these international meetings—at which the U.S. dominates and the rest of the world tries to figure out how to resist—can be critical arenas for the rebuilding of an international Left and the U.S. Left within it.

When was the last time that a multiracial group of U.S. activists got together in a few hours and led a successful protest against our own government and were able to cause the U.S., if only for a moment, international embarrassment and at least some payback for its imperial arrogance? And we did so on the hallowed ground of the South African revolution. For a new generation of left organizers, "I was in the Durban protests against the U.S." may turn out to be one of the many small but significant markers of historical events that can generate multiracial political unity, political and personal trust, and common experiential practice—the historical foundations of a long-hoped-for new movement and new Left.

I will keep you posted.

From the Streets of Alexandra, South Africa: Where is Lenin Now That We Need Him?

The African organizer walks around the community with enormous moral authority. He walks through streets where thousands of youth seem to be standing idle, and almost as many greet him by name. He takes us to the local chamber of commerce, a small office with a few computers, where he embraces the local leadership, and they him. This is the township of Alexandra, one of the poorest and most historically militant townships in greater Johannesburg. He is the local chairperson of the South African Communist Party (SACP), and while he has a formal name he was given at birth, everyone simply calls him Lenin. It's the *nom de guerre* he took when he was forced into exile, where he continued the struggle against the Apartheid regime for many years.

The brutal poverty, the legacy of Apartheid, is starkly present. The dominant form of township housing is still the shanty—small homes one connected to another, often no more than a large, or sometimes small, room. Walls of cinderblocks and bricks, tin roofs of corrugated metal and cement floors are the prevailing architecture. And yet, some have observed, these are still better than in other townships where the housing is even less substantial. In terms of commerce, much of Alexandra looks like the permanently depressed areas of South Central Los Angeles with which I am familiar; the only industries I am able to observe are poorly stocked small convenience stores, nail parlors, and hair salons. Establishments with names like the Chicago Hair Salon and Shoe Repair, with little more than a roof and a few chairs, advertise the latest styles of perms: "the Hollywood," "Black like Me," "Special Feeling," and "Dark and Lovely."

In the midst of Alexandra's 400,000 Black residents, most of whom are living in unbearable poverty, it is the direct organizing, the direct interventions of the Communist Party in general and Lenin in particular, that seem to offer a ray of hope. The local SACP branch, according to Lenin, has an 11 member executive committee and perhaps a few hundred members. At first glance, these are relatively small numbers, but, as always, the discipline of a communist organization with close ties to the masses can geometrically expand that influence.

As we walk through the recently paved roads of Alexandra

(an infrastructure improvement of the ANC government) and past the rows of shanties, we enter a modern two-story brick building with a large inner courtyard. It looks like the housing projects I remember in the South Bronx in the early 1960s, when they were new and clean and before the government refused to maintain them and then blamed the tenants for their disrepair. First, we enter the small offices of the Alexandra branch of the SACP where our delegation of movement organizers from the U.S. is paying a visit. On the blackboard, in carefully printed chalk letters, are notes from a recent political education class on "the land question." They read:

> "*Apartheid is a system of capitalist exploitation, based on colonial and racist forms of domination.*"
>
> "*Addressing this issue must be related to a challenge of building the future society.*"
>
> "*Marxism's essential thesis is the political emergence of an alternative society.*"

In this context Marxism offers hope, in that it confronts economic, political, and spiritual poverty as a temporary condition that can be transformed through political struggle. Alexandra's Lenin improvises from V. I. Lenin's *What is to be Done*: "The communists have aspirations for everyone." And, in an African national liberation struggle in particular, that means reaching out to all classes and all segments of society.

Lenin accompanies us to the local radio station of which the residents are very proud. We walk into the modest but functional offices of ALX FM, Alexandra Community Radio,

"The Station that Empowers You"—with a signal radius of 50 kilometers (approximately 30 miles). The blackboard lists the day's programs:

The Breakfast Show

Gospel

Soul Train

Local Top 20

Young, Black, and Talented

A young Black woman, a local resident, shows up for her volunteer work. She explains, "The NGOs are struggling to get funds, so I am working to gain experience. Someday I hope to get a stipend, but for now I volunteer to get business empowerment." Her favorite program? "The Breakfast Show," where the Communist Party helps to analyze the local, national, and international news. Lenin explains, "if there is a crisis about water, or education, or with the gangs, we are always on the radio keeping the people informed." Lenin agonizes about the crisis of crime in the current period:

> In Alexandra there is very high unemployment, more than 50 percent. Most people do not have jobs. Many young people hijack cars and steal from the community. We are working with the local police to combat the gangs; we carry out community policing. We want to educate the youth and have them put that energy into pressuring the government for more education. But even with the ANC in power, where are the jobs? Where are the social programs?
>
> It is hard making the transition from Apartheid and reactionary capitalism, to democracy and socialism. Let's

look at the gangs today. We are working with the local police to develop a program of community policing. During the Apartheid regime, we carried out a policy of resistance to the laws, making South Africa 'ungovernable.' But now many youth are trying to make the present situation ungovernable, so that every social program we develop can be set back by crime in the community. We cannot build socialism on a foundation of anarchistic destruction. As a member of the Communist Party and as a communist, I am working to rebuild civil society.

Within shouting distance of Alexandra is Sandton, a literal heaven-on-earth for the white elite; 40,000 residents who live in faux Italian villas and other gaudy, affluent architectural styles, cruelly mock the daily lives of the Black masses. As we walk together, Lenin tells the tale of two cities, the past and present class and race conflicts that Alexandra and Sandton represent. During the Apartheid regime, Alexandra residents spent the day working in Sandton as both wage slaves and virtual chattel slaves of the whites. The repressive laws against the workers were so severe that under the pass system, Black workers had a curfew according to which they had to be out of Sandton by dark. They were compelled to return to Alexandra, where they lived in "hostels," prison-like structures with little more than a body-sized cubicle with a concrete floor. The men were segregated into one hostel, and the women into another, so that couples who slaved all day for the white folks could not sleep together or even talk to each other in their time off. "If a husband and wife wanted to see each other, they had to devise means to go back to the rural areas to meet," Lenin explains, each time risking arrest since people's passes were checked by the security forces and violations of the pass law resulted in immediate imprisonment.

Lenin comments on the politics of architecture, the racist and repressive ideology of the built environment under Apartheid:

> The design of every building was politically motivated. The hostels were for hostages. Then the government started building slightly better 'middle class' housing with the WHAM program, 'Winning Hearts and Minds' of the people. Some people living in the government housing did feel superior to the poor, but WHAM could not stop the revolution. In fact, Sandton itself was to show us what white supremacy looked like, for we spent the day cleaning their homes, working in Sandton, but then we had to return to Alexandra to live in squalor.

Lenin goes on to tell us of the historic tradition of struggle in Alexandra—the bus boycott in 1957, directly modeled on the Montgomery bus boycott of 1955. "The bus company tried to raise fares by 100 percent. The people in Alexandra refused and walked miles and miles to Johannesburg for more than four months. Then the bus company dropped its demands and we won."[1] Alexandra has carried on its legacy of struggle into the post-Apartheid era; Lenin points with great pride to a victory that Alexandra residents won against Sandton whites. Sandton, with only 40,000 residents, demanded to be "unlinked" from the nearby 400,000 residents of Alexandra in order to avoid

---

1. For a fascinating look at the parallels between the Montgomery and Alexandra bus boycotts of the 1950s and the current Bus Riders Union campaign in Los Angeles, see Robin D.G. Kelly, "Making History: Everyday Actions of Opposition in the Working Class Struggle for Civil Rights," *AhoraNow* 2 (Spring 1996). Available at www.AhoraNow.org. For a vivid description of Alexandra's pivotal role in the anti-Apartheid struggle from the 1980s until the defeat of Apartheid, see Mzwanele Mayekiso, *Township Politics: Civic Struggles for a New South Africa*, (New York: Monthly Review Press, 1996).

sharing its tax revenues. Alexandra protested that as part of the local municipality act, Sandton was part of the greater Johannesburg council and its taxes had to be shared with the residents of Alexandra. Sandton appealed to the South African Supreme Court that rejected their request and forced them to pay court costs!

The story illustrates the revolutionary nature of demands for democratic rights in an antiracist struggle. Here Blacks took whites to court, and besides the tremendous victory that supported Black majority rule and defeated white gerrymandering, the case illustrated what should never be taken for granted—that Blacks have the legal right to go to court and to win. Only a decade before they could have been arrested, imprisoned or even shot for being on the streets of Sandton after dark. Now, they have legal rights, democratic rights, and Black majority rule—the central demands of the anti-Apartheid revolution.

A Communist's Dilemma:
Left Debate on the Tripartite Alliance

Throughout our trip to South Africa, we have witnessed the first public fissures in the heralded strategic Tripartite Alliance of the African National Congress (ANC), the Congress of South African Trade Unions (COSATU), and the South African Communist Party (SACP).[2] On August 29th and 30th we witnessed, and participated in, the two-day general strike called by COSATU to

---

2. As first mentioned in Dispatch Number 2, the Tripartite Alliance is the most commonly used name for the Revolutionary Alliance formalized in the early 1990s between the ANC, COSATU and the SACP, which grew out of the earlier Congress Alliance of the 1950s.

protest privatization and the dangers of a broader neoliberal agenda.[3] As the rhetoric between the Mbeki government and COSATU heats up, the fight goes beyond a profound disagreement about protecting or privatizing state resources. The fight is the first open challenge to the Alliance itself. In that both COSATU and the SACP do not operate as separate electoral parties, and both agree, so far, to function within the African National Congress, theirs is a struggle to transform the policies of the ANC, the political party that controls the government.

The African National Congress is the majority party in South Africa. Because it is the acknowledged leader of the anti-Apartheid revolution, it has been able to translate that moral authority, as the party of Nelson Mandela, into a powerful electoral party that wins national elections by such a large margin that it does not have to form "coalition governments" with other electoral parties. As an electoral united front, the ANC includes its key constituencies and partners in the Alliance, COSATU and the SACP, both of which have elected their own members to parliament on the ANC electoral slate, some of whom serve in key positions in the ANC governments. But the ANC also has its own structures, its own governance mechanisms, and like all electoral parties, after the elections are over, despite grassroots pressures, it has the power to make policies contrary to the will of the voters and is only accountable to its base at election time.

Many point to the 2002 ANC Party Congress as a key opportunity to challenge the party's direction—where 7,000 elected delegates will either uphold or change the neoliberal

---

3. COSATU and its role in the debate over privatization are discussed at more length in Dispatch Number 2.

wing of the party led by President Thabo Mbeki. The ANC now has key ministers in its government, such as Alec Owen and Trevor Manuel, who are the chief architects and ideologues of privatization; some even call them the International Monetary Fund representatives within the ANC itself. This is in direct contradiction to the left and pro-socialist politics of the ANC's Freedom Charter, as well as the stated politics of COSATU and the SACP. One ANC Leftist argued, "If you read the ANC party program and listen to the public discourse of most ANC members, socialism is the hegemonic ideology." But for organizers on the ground such as Lenin and the masses in Alexandra, what does that matter if the practice is neoliberal?

The "far left," "hard left," or "ultra left" position, depending upon your own mapping of the complex South African political spectrum, is expressed by Oupa Lehulere, an independent Marxist outside of the SACP, who teaches at Khanya College in Johannesburg, a left political education center for workers. Lehulere argues that the two-stage revolution in South Africa should move rapidly from the stage of national liberation to the stage of socialist revolution, and, in his view—given the large Black working class—the Left has failed to use this opportunity.[4] He believes that the COSATU leadership, like the labor bureaucracy of the AFL-CIO, has become materially and politically complicit in capitalist construction. He argues that even its march against privatization was more of a face saving tactical maneuver than a reflection of its

---

4. Oupa Lehulere, interview with the author. Durban, South Africa, September 2001. For a brief discussion of the two-stage revolution in South Africa, see Dispatch Number 2, "The COSATU General Strike," footnote 1.

leadership's politics; many in the COSATU leadership (some
of whom also held high positions in the ANC government) had
previously supported the privatization policies, but felt they
had to respond to the anger of rank and file members who
were facing their consequences. Lehulere observed that as
COSATU and SACP cadre have moved into government positions, some have actually benefited from the selling of state
assets and reaped the material benefits of speculative union
pension funds. "In my view," he said, "the Mbeki government
is so close to U.S. imperialism that South Africa is becoming
the G7½ nation, and is functioning as a sub-imperialist in
Southern Africa." He is sober about the immediate future:
"The SACP is exhausted, they have run out of ideas; they do
not have the political will to challenge Mbeki. It will take a
new workers' movement, a new class consciousness, to break
with the Alliance." He looks to independent workers' movements and independent left collectives, such as those centered
around Khanya College, outside the Alliance, to reshape
South African politics.

Others on the revolutionary Left, typified by Lenin, share
many of the same criticisms of the neoliberal direction of the
Alliance but feel that any efforts to abandon the Alliance at
this point in history are premature and could be disastrous,
leaving the Left out in the cold. Instead, they focus on the
strengthening of left politics inside COSATU and the SACP
and from that base, challenge the ANC leadership and its policies. As Lenin explains:

> Here is our dilemma. The SACP is dedicated to
> building the ANC, but the ANC does not build or help
> to build the SACP. Our people want to struggle, but

Do not want to break the tripartite Alliance.

when we raise criticisms of GEAR [Growth, Employment, And Redistribution, the neoliberal reversal of the ANC's original social democratic Reconstruction and Development Programme (RDP)] we are isolated, marginalized.[5] How do we build protests against the government when SACP members are in such high places? For example, one of the leading advocates of privatization, in fact, the minister of Public Enterprises is Jeff Radebe, a member of the central committee of the SACP. When we in the party challenged privatization, arguing that it brings suffering to the people, he told us that we are 'trapped between a hammer and a sickle,' that is, he redbaited us.

The ANC never voted for privatization, it is not in the ANC program, but it exists in real life. We have to reevaluate the Alliance. We can't breathe within it. The people want to struggle against capitalism. We have to find ways to involve the masses, especially the youth. We are losing membership and credibility. That is why the general strike was so important—if we don't find ways to mobilize the people, both the SACP and COSATU will continue to decline. We talk about national liberation, but our society is remotely controlled by the G7.[6] We understand the need for representative democracy, but the future of socialism is based on participatory democracy. We never voted for the GEAR program. The ministers of the Mbeki government went to a G7 meeting and came back with the GEAR program, and then imposed it on us. In the Freedom Charter, the slogan is 'the people shall govern,' but the people are not governing. Again, that

---

5. For more explanation of GEAR and RDP, see Dispatch Number 2, footnote 5.

6. G7 is used here to refer to the world's seven most economically powerful countries: the United States, Canada, England, France, Germany, Italy and Japan (not including Russia, whose addition makes the grouping the G8).

is where the SACP can help lead, to create participatory democracy in communities like Alexandra.

Those inside the ANC structures of governance are passionate in their explanations of the constraints they face and the true
historical victories of the ANC, as well as their critique of the
one-note tone of their critics who often downplay the profound
victory, past and present, of the antiracist revolution and the national liberation struggle.

Many of those directly involved in government feel that the
Left—even their own friends and comrades in the grassroots
movements, the SACP and COSATU—does not understand the
pressures they are under from South African and international
capitalists and the compromises they must make to prevent South
Africa from falling into social chaos.

The ANC faces the dilemma of determining what a progressive public policy and program looks like in a world dominated
by the United States. Michael Sachs, a researcher for the ANC
and one of our hosts, gave the following explanation of the ANC
Left's strategic dilemmas, and implicitly, a defense against their
left, or "ultra left," critics.[7] Sachs explained the fundamental strategic framework that the ANC leadership feels should shape the
debates about policy and strategy: The ANC came to power as
the result of a negotiated settlement with the South African

---

7. Michael Sachs, who is a figure in his own right, is the son of Albie Sachs, one of
the many heroes of the anti-Apartheid resistance, who, like the late Joe Slovo,
served as the general secretary of the South African Communist Party. The Slovo
and Sachs families reflect the prominent and courageous role that some Jews have
played among the antiracist whites in South Africa. See Glenn Frankel, *Rivonia's
Children: Three Families and the Cost of Conscience in White South Africa* (New
York: Farrar, Straus and Giroux, 1999).

Apartheid regime, in particular, and the West in general. Obviously, had there been a full-scale seizure of power, the product of an armed struggle by the Black majority, there would have been less compromise. But such a revolution, in his view, was not historically possible at the time, especially without the protection and countervailing power of the Soviet Union. A guerilla army would have had to overthrow the militarily advanced and brutal Apartheid state and, most likely, the armed intervention of the U.S. CIA and military as well.

While many have criticized former President Mandela and his successor, President Mbeki, for their focus on "sending positive signals to Western markets," Sachs emphasized, "we don't want another Chile here," that is, a U.S. instigated military coup against the democratic ANC government. (Henry Kissinger, who was U.S. Secretary of State at the time of the coup against Allende, explained later that if the people mistakenly vote for socialism, the U.S. has the obligation to forcibly overturn their decision.) In the context of that past history and in the wake of the strikes on the World Trade Center and Pentagon and the threats of the Bush administration to wage a "war without boundaries," we must take seriously the belief of the ANC leadership that they have restricted capacity for actual self-determination. Sachs argued, "Despite the difficult international balance of forces, the ANC government is able to take international positions independent of the United States because we don't owe our soul to the World Bank, we have carefully avoided international debt."

If the ANC agrees it came to power to "manage capitalism" but also agrees that its overall program is socialist in general orientation, then a facile discussion about whether South Africa is "ready" for a socialist revolution—which all parties in this debate agree it is not—still masks the profound historical choices in the present between a left social democratic governmental strategy to constrain capitalism and a neoliberal one to unleash the free market.

One ANC official told me that it really might be historically necessary for COSATU and the SACP to try to form a labor party and run independent candidates for parliament. Perhaps in that context, Mbeki and the ANC would feel pressure from the Left as well as the Right, especially if the new labor party won enough seats to require the ANC to form a "coalition government." Others have argued that such a move would be disastrous, and asked, "Why should we give up the ANC that we, as communists, have built for decades? Why should we be forced out?" Instead, they have talked about running their candidates for the ANC Party Congress in 2002.

At an important public forum during the World Conference Against Racism, sponsored by the ANC, Blade Nzimande, the general secretary of the SACP who is also a high ranking ANC official, responded to left criticisms of the neoliberal direction of the ANC government and the charges that the SACP is complicit in those policies. When challenged from the audience, "Why doesn't the SACP leave the ANC government and help form an independent labor party?" Nzimande replied, "because there is no relevant political life outside of the Alliance." He agreed that perhaps the SACP, in its efforts to hold the Alliance together, had not put forth an independent socialist politics, and proposed that communists needed to develop a more clearly defined "minimum program" that is, a left, transitional program towards socialism to help counter the neoliberal direction of the ANC. On the other hand, he expressed concern that the SACP should not risk isolation within the ANC united front. Given what he believed is the grave and continued danger of white reactionaries, Black conservatives, and international imperialism, "protecting and defending the democratic revolution and the Strategic Alliance" is the central task.

As various left forces debate the relative merits and tactics of their participation in the Tripartite Alliance and struggle among themselves as to how to move the Alliance to the Left, there are right-wing forces in the ANC led by a growing Black bourgeoisie, who have threatened the SACP and COSATU that they will move to break the Alliance by pushing them out. Some from the Right Wing have declared that because of COSATU's general strike and the growing public criticism of the Mbeki government, "the Alliance is dead." Whether or not that is a spontaneous comment or an orchestrated opening from even higher sources in the ANC, is open to debate. But it is a signal that for all the forces in the Alliance, the level of internal and public struggle is escalating.

Within the South African Communist Party there is also struggle over the organization's direction. Several SACP cadre shared with me their worry that the party is becoming isolated from some of the most oppressed and desperate sectors of the South African working class, especially the rural proletariat and peasantry. They pointed to the growing movement of landless people who had been promised land by the ANC Freedom Charter but are presently on the verge of starvation and homelessness. This movement held a mass protest, led by the Durban Social Forum, against the ANC government the day after the COSATU general strike with the slogan, "You promised us land and you gave us jail." The Pan African Congress (PAC), a Black nationalist organization outside of the Alliance is a leading force in the landless movement. Whatever criticisms and disagreements the SACP has with PAC, and they are profound, SACP supporters saw the rise of the PAC leadership and the absence of SACP leadership in the landless movement as another sign of danger.

Lenin, for one, believes the Communist Party must push the ANC government to take a more aggressive policy on the re-distribution of land to the Black masses:

> We have to change the legacy of Apartheid, not adjust to the legacy of Apartheid. We have to wage war to get our land back, a careful war, a strategic war, but a war nonetheless. The ANC Freedom Charter said, "the land shall belong to those who work it." This land was taken from us by force, we have to find ways to go beyond the Land Restitution Act for a massive transfer of land to Black people who are hungry for the land that was once theirs.

Chris Hani, the former General Secretary of the South African Communist Party who was assassinated in 1993, looms large in the popular imagination. Hani was a popular, charismatic, loved mass leader of the SACP and ANC who, sensing the growing capitalist pressures on the anti-Apartheid transition to power, announced that he would not seek office in any ANC government. Instead, he would lead mass movements to advance the politics of the Black working class and workers of all races, to keep the government honest and moving to the left. He was assassinated by Afrikaner racist forces (as Amilcar Cabral was assassinated by Portuguese agents just before the national liberation movement in Guinea Bissau took power).

It is hard to imagine or understand the essential historical role of charismatic "maximum leaders" like Dr. King, Malcolm X, or

Nelson Mandela, and yes, Chris Hani in shaping historical possibilities. Mass movements win or lose in general because of material economic and political conditions, but each mass movement urgently needs key leaders that the people believe are the match for, or even superior to, their opponents. The assassination of Chris Hani is mourned every day by the South African Left, because it is understood that he could present a mass challenge to Mbeki; his "out of governance" power would have put enormous popular pressure on the policies of neoliberalism.

If the forces of transnational capital are placing tremendous pressure on the ANC government, which they are, the SACP's leadership of mass struggles is critical to counteract that pressure and to "defend and extend the anti-Apartheid democratic revolution." That is why the highly visible SACP leadership in the COSATU strike was seen as encouraging and necessary, and that is why it was received with such antagonism by the Mbeki government. In terms of greater unity between the SACP leadership and rank and file, the SACP issued a very strong statement on August 30, 2001, the day of the COSATU general strike:

> The success of the general strike is a clear and strong message to the bosses and government that privatization is not the route to go. Today's strike was also a conscious offensive against capitalism itself and the building of a people's economy that meets our people's basic needs, develops infrastructure, and creates new, quality, and sustainable jobs... To those who attacked the SACP in the run up to the strike, today's general strike sends them a clear message that instead of the SACP being caught between a hammer and a sickle as they alleged, the SACP is firmly united in its struggle against privatization. In any case, it is a thousand times better to be caught between a

hammer and a sickle than to hang our necks on the apron strings of the bourgeoisie and its economic policies.[8]

These are stirring words, but, given their enormous constraints, will the SACP be able to make the transition from marches and declarations to actual changes in ANC policy? Lenin and his colleagues are proposing the aggressive creation of a socialist politics, rooted in the Black working class, that becomes a visible, powerful and public force in the daily life of the entire society—visible to the average worker, to the employed and unemployed on the streets of Alexandra, and to the ANC government. Creating this force requires powerful, militant, socialist, and revolutionary organizing from below and a complex policy of both unity and struggle with the existing order. Otherwise, the slogan of the SACP and many COSATU supporters, "Socialism is the Future, Build it Now" will regress to a hollow reformism "tipping its hat to socialism."

As many South Africans look toward the 2002 ANC Party Congress as the sight of a major showdown and a way to measure the relative strength of all the forces, many questions are being generated: Will the ANC right wing continue to effectively berate and intimidate the SACP and COSATU? Will there be an electoral insurgency against Mbeki, not to remove him but to push a very hard program in a socialist direction in a clear rebuke to the neoliberal policies? Even if so, how can COSATU and SACP enforce the implementation of such a program—in that the ANC government and the Mbeki faction have clearly ignored past resolutions against privatization?

---

8. SACP, "The People Have Spoken," Statement of the South African Communist Party, 30 August 2001.

Does the SACP envision any life outside of the Alliance and does it have democratic mechanisms by which the rank and file cadre on the ground can have influence over party policy inside and outside the ANC? Can the SACP continue to lead mass struggles against the Mbeki government when the SACP is also serving in the ANC government and some of the government's key ministers are members of the SACP? And if so, would it risk greater, if possibly only temporary, marginalization or even expulsion to push a left independent program against privatization for greater South African independence from world financial markets and U.S. hegemony?

The SACP, in an effort to avoid sectarianism, has told the public that once inside government, the Communist Party will abide by ANC structures and decisions. But why does the SACP hold itself to rules that no others follow—for any mass political party has factions, caucuses, and debates? Why can't the SACP go into the ANC with an open and aboveboard left program for ANC policy? And given the profound differences between SACP ministers and SACP organizers on the ground like Lenin, how does the party resolve its internal line struggles to reach a unified political plan of action?

From the South African Revolution to the U.S. Left: Lessons I Take Home

For many Leftists in South Africa (fortunately, at every level of South African society there are many Leftists), the crisis in the Alliance goes beyond disagreement over the neoliberal policies of the government. It extends to whether independent political action on the part of the South African working class can impact and change those policies. Despite every effort to assuage, cajole, and further subsidize white South African and foreign capital, there has been massive capital flight from the country and an estimated one million jobs lost, many from the decently paid and unionized industrial sector. Moreover, while the government admits that in the "medium term" there will be further loss of jobs, they are placing their hopes on "the knowledge economy" and the high tech sector, which most concede will only benefit the already super-privileged white professional South Africans, among the former perpetrators of, and/or willing accomplices to, Apartheid.

In the eight years since the ANC came to power, the once vital civic associations that courageously helped to lead the anti-Apartheid revolution have declined and in some areas virtually disintegrated, replaced by less mass based, less confrontational, and often factionalized NGOs. (The analogies with the post-1970s decline in the militancy and mass character of the Black liberation and civil rights movement in the U.S. are painfully evident.) COSATU and the SACP made the decision to send many of their top cadre into the ANC government. Given that one ideological pillar of white, Christian, Western imperialism and Apartheid was the myth that Black Africans cannot govern themselves, the ANC's development of a conscientious, honest, and capable state bureaucracy was essential. A social movement that transformed itself into an electoral party like the ANC cannot fight for state power, no matter how partial, without giving high priority to the actual running of the government unless one wants a coalition of the Afrikaners, the British, and the Inkatha Freedom Party and their supporters to retake power. Given the Communist Party's commitment to building the ANC and its government and consolidating the anti-Apartheid revolution, it was understandable that it would decide to help build those structures by contributing some of its most influential cadre.

Still, this division of labor also created a major contradiction. Many socialists and revolutionaries can agree, at least in theory, that under certain historical circumstances, it may be a good tactical move to send some communists into a bourgeois democratic capitalist government—based on theories of representative democracy, and especially in the context of an unfinished revolution for national liberation and a government based on Black majority rule. But the more fundamental tenet of Marxism is that at all times in history it is strategically central to the communists' unique role to advance the democratic and socialist aspirations of the masses, based on the building of grassroots mass movements. This can only be done by building revolutionary consciousness and organization among the working and oppressed classes at the point of production and in their communities. This is especially true when ANC spokespeople honestly and correctly assess that "we inherited a capitalist economy and society and our job is to administer capitalism in the best and most progressive way possible—we are not a socialist organization."

The unique responsibility of a communist party to lead the open struggle for socialism is also consistent with the SACP's theory of a two-stage revolution, the first stage for national liberation, democracy and Black majority rule (an amazing achievement in itself) and the second stage to simultaneously prevent capitalist and racist counterrevolution and advance towards a socialist transformation, and eventually, a socialist revolution. This strategy of a two-stage revolution was critical to the victory of the Russian and Chinese revolutions and, in my view, is clearly vindicated in the South African historical reality. The ANC and the SACP deserve the admiration of people throughout the world for leading a broad united front to defeat Apartheid—a popular democratic revolution led by all classes of the Black population in alliance with a multiracial movement of all progressive South Africans. That was their greatest historical achievement.

The question is what happens after the victory of the anti-Apartheid revolution, when the first stage includes the inheritance of a wealthy capitalist economy, with a powerful white South African bourgeoisie with very strong ties to international imperialism. For someone like Alexandra's Lenin, the argument is not that the South African Communist Party or the left wing of COSATU must somehow push the South African working class into a socialist revolution whether it wants it or not. Although the dream of socialism is popular, after centuries of fighting against colonialism, many Black workers do want some way to consolidate gains in their lives. And, no matter how critical many are of Mbeki, he is a Black president in a Black-run government. The dilemma is how the South African Left can develop a class-based politics still rooted in national liberation traditions and intensify struggle with the growing Black bourgeois leadership, while building a broad united front against U.S. and Western imperialism.

All eyes are on South Africa as it fights for its life and confronts challenges that are far more advanced than any of us in the U.S. Left can even fathom, let alone know how to resolve.

As the South Africans struggle for self-determination, the Bush administration is moving with bipartisan support to try to institutionalize a permanent war economy and a permanent war posture. But, no matter how ominous and how truly powerful, the U.S. government is not omnipotent, and a worldwide democratic front for peace and national liberation is even more necessary under the present conditions.

I have had the honor of visiting a far more democratic South Africa than anything we have experienced in our own country. In South Africa, Black Africans are debating their own destiny and they trust us from the U.S. Left enough to include us in a discussion that has profound impact on the world Left. For several of us—inspired by the everyday intelligence and honesty of every strata of Black African leadership and the powerful public role of a socialist-oriented Black working class reaching out to build a multiracial movement—there was the romantic and strategic desire to see if we could move to South Africa to help, in any way we could, with the protection and advancement of the South African revolution. But even before the epochal shift in world history provoked, but not caused, by the strikes on the World Trade Center and Pentagon, it became clear to me that my, and our, role cannot be evaded. We live in the belly of the beast and our historical obligation is to do everything we can to stay the hand of brutality that our government imposes on most of the world's people—including our new friends and comrades in South Africa.

Just one specific example. While we were at the World Conference Against Racism, the United States announced that it was accusing the South African government and many others, including Japan, of "dumping" steel in the U.S. at prices below its costs, and was going to a WTO court to ask for tariffs of 300 percent against South African steel; this would of course prevent any such imports into the United States. Now, here is the world superpower—that tries to shove its products, its ideology, and its social system down the throats of every nation in the world, breaking down tariff barriers in nations it wants to penetrate and simultaneously erecting them in the U.S.—unable to compete in the "free market" with South African steel. South Africa needs those exports to gain foreign exchange, to build up its infrastructure, and to protect itself from the "IMF loan shark," as Ibo Mandaza from Zimbabwe so aptly called it.

Just as it was during the Vietnam war, the main contribution and responsibility of the U.S. Left is to challenge the policies and institutions of our own government and to demand a "hands off South Africa" movement to allow self-determination in South Africa no matter what direction its people choose. For those of us in the U.S. who want to offer concrete material aid to the South African revolution, we should organize to oppose the U.S. attacks on South African imports. This will also involve taking on the chauvinist United Steelworkers Union that has tied itself completely to its own bosses with a protectionist "stand up for steel" campaign (that has been endorsed by "free trader" Bush). This concrete reflection of "hands off South Africa" will challenge progressives and Leftists in the AFL-CIO.

In the midst of a sea of darkness, as the U.S. government threatens to bomb the world and, ironically, drive its own society back to the stone age, it is encouraging to see grassroots leaders like Lenin in Alexandra and the left COSATU leadership throughout South Africa, working to rebuild the national liberation and socialist struggle on the ground. For the organizer, life is fundamentally optimistic—there are people to see, mobilizations to organize, protests and strikes, internal and external struggles. On the ground, the people have only two choices right now: to struggle or to perish. For Lenin and his friends, that is not even a question to contemplate, they are too busy organizing. For whatever the resolution of the agonizing and historically pivotal strategic debates in South Africa, it is the Lenins of the world who are the ultimate drivers of history—in South Africa and the U.S.

I will keep you posted.

Dispatch Number

May 1, 2002
LOS ANGELES

The World Conference Against Racism: A Strategic Sum-Up

On September 11, 2001, a Black man from Harlem, an NGO delegate to the just concluded World Conference Against Racism (WCAR), was returning home to New York when his plane was detoured to Newfoundland, where he and his fellow passengers were detained for several days. The symbolism was painfully reflective of the conference from which he was just returning, for Newfoundland had been attacked, not discovered, in 1497, by Giovanni Caboto, an Italian sailor backed by the English Crown. The English called their stolen treasure "new found land" only to subjugate the indigenous Mi'Kmaq people

and kill all the Beothuk. It was not just a few delegates from
WCAR who were driven off course and detained on September
11, 2001. It felt like the whole conference and all we had
worked for was being eclipsed by a shadow of reaction. Seemingly overnight, the Bush Administration and the two-party elite
were able to use the events of September 11 to move against
any vestiges of progressivism and liberalism—let alone radicalism, anti-imperialism, and socialism—that they hadn't already
beaten out of the body politic over the past two decades. The
U.S. Republicans and Democrats have formed a unity party; the
Left's accusation that there is only one capitalist party with two
branches is no longer debated, as there is "bipartisan" support
for racial profiling, massive expenditures for the military, restrictions on already limited civil rights and civil liberties, wholesale
layoffs of workers, and a war hysteria that the Bush Administration is trying to institutionalize. In every historical
circumstance, there is a challenge to the Left. In this situation,
the challenge is how to build a movement against war, racism,
and imperialist expansion in the midst of the most bellicose and
reactionary mass politics.

Robin Kelley, in his foreword, compares WCAR to the 1955
Bandung Conference of Non-Aligned Nations in terms of historical significance. The actual historical impact of an event depends
upon the actions, events, and consequences that follow it; the
writing of the "historical record" is an organizing project, a reflection of class struggle and national liberation struggles. We are
all actors in making history, and the writing of it is one form of
its making. Walter Benjamin, a German antifascist revolutionary,
commented on the Right's efforts to smash the history of the
Left's victories: "Only that historian will have the gift of fanning

the spark of hope in the past who is firmly convinced that even the dead will not be safe from the enemy if he wins."[1] The organized Right, including far too many self-promoting or disillusioned former "sixties radicals," is constructing a mass amnesia about the enormous victories of the U.S. and world Left during the "two decades of the sixties."[2] The struggle to put WCAR back on the agenda begins with the reconstruction of the historical record.

The events that have unfolded since September 11 make a thoughtful sum-up of the World Conference Against Racism even more important than it was in the days immediately following WCAR. To move on, without considering the deep and strategic connection between the two events, would be a grave mistake. At this point in history, reconstructing an ideological, political, organizational, and tactical unity for a not yet created antiracist, anti-imperialist U.S. Left is the central challenge facing the disparate if courageous social movements in this country. Durban, WCAR, and the Non-Governmental Organization (NGO) Forum in particular, created an important laboratory for assessing the actual state of these movements and their efforts to impact a world event of great possibility. If there is ever to be an effective anti-war movement in the U.S., it must be tied to the development of a viable international antiracist,

---

1. Walter Benjamin, "Thesis on the Philosophy of History," in *Illuminations*, trans. Harry Zohn, (1938; New York: Scocken Books, 1969) 255.

2. Especially for a younger generation that did not live through those epochal events, I use the term "two decades of the sixties" to refer to the period, arbitrarily constructed, from 1955, the time of the Bandung Conference and the Montgomery Bus Boycott to 1975, the defeat of the U.S. in Vietnam. I would mark, again arbitrarily, the counter-revolution against the gains of the New Left as 1980, with the election of Ronald Reagan.

anti-imperialist united front. The story of WCAR must be told as part of that process. This is one such effort.

The final governmental document coming out of Durban and the brazen U.S. walk out from the entire conference clearly demonstrates that the antiracist forces at Durban did not win many concrete demands. Still, as a dress rehearsal for future world struggles, WCAR was an important and, at times, amazing event, the high points of which were the complete disgrace and isolation of the United States government and its self-exposure as a racist bully, the spirited show of support for the Palestinian liberation struggle, and the strong NGO document against racism—even if rejected in its essence by the world's governments.

At every point in history, left forces must judge their progress, achievements, and failures against some barometer of what is historically possible given the actual balance of power. There was no way a disparate array of groups from around the world, many of whom had no previous history of working together, could have imposed their will on their own governments, let alone a world body dominated by the U.S. The low point of Durban was the recognition of the generally disorganized and ineffective state of progressives working within the UN structures, demonstrated by the inability of any forms, structures, or political forces to provide political or organizational leadership. The historic significance of Durban will depend largely on post-Durban initiatives to move history forward, initiatives that are desperately needed and for which this strategic sum-up can provide a point of reference for debate, discussion, re-examination, regrouping, and reconstruction. Thus, this book is a tactic within a larger antiracist organizing strategy.

When I first knew I was going to Durban, I planned to participate in and analyze two separate but interrelated conferences—the UN Governmental World Conference Against Racism, and the WCAR NGO Forum, a meeting of non-governmental organizations held the week before the governments met, ostensibly to impact governmental deliberations. In fact, this narrative focuses almost exclusively on the NGO Forum for several interrelated reasons: 1) my own work focuses on the building of radical and, if possible, revolutionary movements to challenge existing state and corporate structures; 2) the NGO Forum was so badly organized and so ineffective on its own terms that it was unable to actually impact the UN governmental conference; these were fundamentally two separate events that theoretically needed to be interconnected but in practice were not; 3) the UN Governmental Conference did everything it could to exclude participation of the NGO delegates—denying credentials, denying press passes to established media if they were also delegates from NGOs, and denying access to the conference, even as observers, for the thousand or so delegates from the NGO Forum who stayed in Durban for the second week.

In this chapter, I will summarize the main strategic debates and developments at the NGO Forum and evaluate WCAR on its own terms and stated objectives.

The U.S. Threat

Malcolm X often repeated his threat to take Black peoples' grievances against the United States to the United Nations on the grounds that Black people had inalienable national rights as an oppressed people, and had demands for autonomy and equality that went beyond civil rights granted in the U.S. constitution.

argued for going to UN for demands.

These were "human rights" that were protected by international law, and were best won in an international arena. Despite Malcolm's agitational threat, there was, in fact, no concerted effort to go to the UN. Everyone in the Civil Rights Movement and Black Liberation Movement understood that the UN was not and could not be an "independent" institution. It was located in New York, "U.S.A." The United States was the most powerful world superpower at the time, and the U.S. and the European colonial powers dominated the Security Council. Still, how times have changed. Malcolm's thinking was shaped by a revolutionary period in which every year contained events of such historical import that they seemed like decades. The Soviet Union and the Eastern bloc nations provided a military and even nuclear counterbalance to the U.S.; the revolutionary movements in the Third World were distinctly anti-U.S., anti-imperialist, and generally pro-socialist, and the U.S. was painfully aware of some of the limits of its own power, even its need to curry favor with Third World governments to prevent them from "going communist."

Despite the structural obstacles, Malcolm did indeed carry out his UN strategy. He organized one of the most important events in 20th century antiracist history—his brilliant alliance with Fidel Castro to bring the Cuban communist leader to the Hotel Theresa in Harlem, after he heard that the Cuban delegation had been pushed around and discriminated against in a midtown luxury hotel near the UN at the instigation of the U.S. government. For days, Cuban revolutionaries, many of them Black, and Black activists from Harlem held a love fest—infuriating the U.S. government, whose move had backfired. The famous pictures of Fidel and Malcolm talking strategy to each other in the heart of Harlem were sent around the world. This was an embryonic but profound expression of the same strategy articulated in *Dispatches*: build a strategic alliance of the multinational multiracial working class inside the U.S. with oppressed peoples and nations both inside and outside the U.S. to directly challenge U.S. imperialism.

But WCAR took place in an age of world counter-revolution, 40 years later, in what seems like light years later, in which the former Soviet Union no longer exists, Malcolm X, Martin Luther King Jr., Fred Hampton, Mark Clark and too many other Black leaders in the U.S. have been assassinated, the vast majority of Third World nations have been recolonized into the most blatant form of economic and political dependency, and the U.S., now the unchecked "rogue superpower," is throwing its weight around the world with the greatest imperial arrogance. And this was *before* September 11.

Throughout WCAR, before and after the U.S. walk-out, the United States was aggressively pushing its objectives and had enormous influence with, or upon, virtually every government in the world. Within the Third World especially, the level of economic dependency, fear of U.S. military intervention, and even cultural subordination made a coordinated resistance to U.S. domination very difficult. The U.S. understands the role of ideology. It tries to rule by intellectual and ideological hegemony when possible and brute force only when persuasion and voluntary self-servitude fail. The U.S. approaches each UN conference as a tactic in its broader strategy of world rule. Thus, despite the weakness of many of the actual antiracist organizations at WCAR, the sum total of their work was still effective enough to momentarily drive the U.S. off a world stage. Clearly, it does not like to be criticized, let alone attacked. The U.S. was uniquely and profoundly vulnerable at the World Conference Against Racism because of its history of racism, which is not only reflected in the vicious ideology of white supremacy, but also in the fundamental structures of capitalist and later imperialist conquest—genocide, slavery, mass torture, and murder. The myth of white, Christian, European capitalist superiority is central to the master narrative of the U.S. nation-state and its historical justification for its manifest destiny. As such, the antiracist movement in general and the movement for reparations in particular are enormous threats to U.S. ideological hegemony. This history, once exposed, shows Western civilization as Western barbarism and calls into question the very historical right of the "United" States to exist.

Thus, whether through its own direct threats and influence or working through its proxies in Europe such as the pathetic Belgians (with their own nation also built upon African genocide), the U.S. took WCAR and its potential outcomes very seriously.[3] As a result, the efforts of the U.S. to intimidate Third World nations was a prominent theme at Durban; it threatened dependent governments to stay away from criticisms of Israel, and to disassociate themselves from support for Palestine and reparations, or suffer the consequences.

This UN conference attracted a group of self-selected antiracist NGOs, many with ties to actual struggles on the

---

3. The story of Belgian "slave labor" and "mass murder" in the cruelly named Congo Free State or as it was once called "the Belgian Congo" and the account of one of the first anti-colonial movements inside a Western imperialist nation is told by Adam Hochschild, *King Leopold's Ghost* (New York: Houghton Mifflin, 1999).

ground. In that context, the efforts of the majority of NGO delegates to push a strong antiracist agenda, and in particular the work of those who tried to directly focus on the link between racism and Western imperialism provided a strategic challenge that shaped the entire conference. The central contradiction at Durban was between the United States and the G8 nations on the one hand and the world antiracist movement on the other. And this time, the antiracist movement *was* choosing the United Nations as an important site of struggle.

Decoding the United Nations

At its heart, the World Conference against Racism should be understood as the *United Nations* Conference Against Racism, only a part of which was the NGO Forum. Many on the antiracist Left see the United Nations as a marginal or even irrelevant site of struggle. The UN General Assembly, the institution's most democratic structure, allows each nation one vote; but because of Security Council permanent member veto power (held by the U.S., Britain, China, Russia and France) any resolutions that challenge the U.S., the G8, or their allies can be roadblocked. And yet, the UN creates an organizational opportunity for diverse forces to coalesce, debate, and negotiate. In its international aspirations, its structures of public debate on the behavior of the United States, its progressive world conferences—antiracism, environment, development, women, HIV/AIDS, human rights, children and poverty—the UN offers a ray of hope for many Third World nations. In the absence of a Non-Aligned Movement with its own structures, a world Left, or a socialist or communist international, the UN reflects the potential and the limits of the G77 and China (the nations of the Global South) and the actual balance of forces in the world.[4]

The NGOs—Situating a Resistance in a Structure of Accommodation

The world governments reflected in the UN have, over the last 25 years, supported an expanded role for NGOs, corresponding to the decline and fall of many state socialist governments. The ideological focus on "civil society" and NGOs (along with the transnational corporations) as "civil society players" comes out of anticommunist theories that critique many of the totalitarian forms of state socialist experiments but never acknowledge the dictatorial tendencies and realities of capitalism as well. The NGOs play an ideological role in the new neoliberal world, in which capitalist governments in structural alignment with the corporate class try to create the illusion that they are impacted by the democratic interaction of "civil society players."[5]

The UN, whose processes for years were restricted to governments only, has opened up many of its processes to include

---

4. The United Nations is organized into many different blocs of countries: the United States often functions as a caucus of one, the European Union as one block, and the G77 and China as another. The Group of 77 (G77) represents all the nations of the Global South or Third World, and in actuality contains more than 130 individual nations.

5. For a critique of the co-optive process and the myths involving NGO's, see Eric Mann, *Grassroots Strategies for Bali and Johannesburg: Confronting Corporate Power at the World Summit on Sustainable Development* (Los Angeles: Strategy Center Publications, 2002) available from www.thestrategycenter.org.

NGO and "civil society" participation, if only at the most minimal and often tokenistic levels of "input." Right now, the UN governments are not that worried about the critiques by NGO structures because, frankly, many of the NGOs are poorly organized, represent little or no social base, have voluntarily accepted accommodationist politics or are directly funded by their own governments, or other governments. Many Third World NGOs are funded by the European Union and U.S. Agency for International Development (USAID) or by the UN itself. Many Third World NGOs cannot afford to get to UN meetings without stipends from the UN. These ties that bind, as one can imagine, create a material constraint on their behavior once they arrive.

Outside of the UN context, the NGO phenomenon is under sharp critique by independent social movements, grassroots groups, left trade unions, and national liberation movements—that is, any intellectual or group that is situated in opposition to world racism and imperialism. James Petras, an expert on Latin American revolutionary movements, accuses the NGOs as a whole of being "agents of imperialism," siding with their governments to undermine radical and revolutionary movements, and putting forth an "anti-state" ideology that fosters the myth that there is a big world of "civil society" in which the poor and the rich interact democratically. In that way, the NGOs function to leave the capitalist state relatively immune from attack.[6]

---

6. James Petras, "Imperialism and NGOs in Latin America," *Monthly Review*, 49 (1997): 10-27.

The noted Palestinian intellectual, Edward Said, expresses similar views, criticizing the Palestinian NGOs for their objective opposition to genuine national liberation:

> Put very simply are they a substitute for a political movement, and can they ever become one? I don't think so since each operates in a bilateral relationship with the funders, each of whom makes clear that money for work on democracy, health care, education—all important things—is forthcoming only within the overall frame of the current peace process [which the Palestinian Intifada is rejecting]. And these NGOs, necessary as they are to keep Palestinian life going, themselves become the goal, instead of, for example, liberation, or ending the occupation, or changing Palestinian society.[7]

Given these historically-determined constraints, many militant, radical, and even revolutionary forces have accepted the technical definition of a non-governmental organization while simultaneously distancing themselves from the dominant history and culture of an NGO structure they are trying to impact.

At WCAR, while there was awareness of the dangers of the NGO phenomenon, many of the delegates were not "regulars" at UN events, but had come to Durban out of a passion to fight racism and just to have said that they had been there. There is a radical edge to the fight against racism, rooted in the abuses that people of color all over the world have suffered and continue to suffer, that exerted a powerful impact on the general category of NGO and attracted a more militant and independent cross-section of grassroots groups. This

---

7. Edward Said, *The End of the Peace Process* (New York: Vintage Books, 2001), xx.

is not to say that careerism, funder-driven behavior, and "going along with the program" dynamics were not present at Durban, but they were not at all the dominant tendency.

While the NGOs still ranged over a wide spectrum of politics, as a group, they had come to Durban to launch a historic challenge to world racism—not through sit-ins or take-overs or armed struggle, but in the equally important arena of ideological struggle, in the battle over the language of resolutions. The primary goal of the NGO Forum was to draft a strong document to influence the subsequent UN governmental conference and its final declaration and program—with the understanding that the antiracist movement in the world, reflected in mass organizations or even "advocacy organizations," was far more militant and concerned about the structural causes of, and cures for, racist policies than most of the world's governments. Thus, Durban was a world workshop to evaluate the capacity of the NGOs to impact the policies of the UN.

Many NGOs from the United States, especially those from the Black Liberation Movement and Civil Rights Movement, were aware of the efforts of Malcolm X (and some were aware of the prior efforts by W.E.B. Dubois and Paul Robeson decades before) to bring the antiracist and national self-determination demands of Black people to the UN. But in reality, very few groups had really tested the UN as a forum for moving public debate forward, or tested the capacity of any international body to get the outlaw and racist West to 'fess up to its past sins, let alone force the U.S. and Europe to begin a process of introspection, repentance, and reparation.

The Historical Opportunity—Based on Time, Place, and Conditions

Given the organizational structure of the UN, and the actual state of the antiracist forces worldwide, what could the delegates from the non-governmental organizations, expect to achieve?

☐ We might expect to coalesce progressive antiracist forces. Many city-wide and regional groups in the United States, the most viable grassroots organizations with any base on the ground, have very little experience in international networking and relationship building. The UN provides an efficient way to meet people from all over the world, in one centralized venue and to learn from each other. This conference, focused on racism, would draw together some of the most progressive NGOs.

☐ We might be able to unite in the production of an NGO Forum Declaration, a unifying progressive antiracist statement of policy and demands that could function as an ideological instrument on its own terms and generate a focused and prioritized set of key demands to raise against the Western powers.

☐ We might expect to unify as many of the 10,000 NGO delegates as possible around an antiracist NGO document, and then try to exercise influence on the governmental document. Even if rejected by the US and G8 the actual movements on the ground could come out of the process strengthened with greater international moral and political authority. That would require producing a high-visibility document, the NGO Forum Declaration, a manifesto of antiracist, anti-imperialist resistance that could be circulated throughout the world, and among each group's home constituencies.

☐ We might expect to create networks of cooperation among the NGOs, both outside and inside UN structures, forged in the process of struggle that could continue after the Durban conference to place even greater pressure on transnational corporations and governments in subsequent months and years.

The idea of using the WCAR as a "court of public opinion" is not utopian. At the past two UN World Conferences to Combat Racism and Racial Discrimination (both in Geneva, in 1978 and 1983), the antiracist forces focused their efforts on toppling the Apartheid regime in South Africa. As a tactic, the UN forums played a positive role in an overall international strategy by the African National Congress (ANC) to isolate and eventually bring down the racist government and achieve Black majority rule. The 1983 conference declared "Apartheid is totally abhorrent to the dignity of mankind and a threat to international peace and security."[8] (The United States boycotted those conferences as well.)

It was possible at Durban that the NGOs and some progressive governments developed a mass antiracist mass initiative with a foundation of support for reparations and Palestinian national liberation. But such a forceful antiracist initiative would

---

8. South Africa Human Rights Commission, "Countdown to World Conference," <http://sahrc.org.sa.za/count_down_to_world conference.htm> (accessed 1 August 2002).

have required an international movement at a far higher level of consciousness and organization than presently exists. A few of the problems faced by the NGO forces and the NGO Forum illustrate this gap between an ideal plan and the actual practice at Durban.

Structural Opportunity for Leadership

Every United Nations conference on a major issue, such as WCAR, has a complex but relatively orderly process by which a series of preparatory committees—PrepComs—are organized, at which governmental delegations argue over policy issues, write draft language, debate, bargain, and negotiate toward a final document. In anticipation of Durban, Regional PrepComs were held in Europe (Strasbourg, France), the Americas (Santiago, Chile), Africa (Dakar, Senegal), and Asia/Middle East (Tehran, Iran). These regional meetings were supposed to feed their results into full international PrepComs at Geneva. NGO activists were present at all of those meetings. The point? That there was plenty of opportunity to develop a functional leadership to provide structure and guidance to the antiracist NGOs in Durban.

At WCAR, an official UN structure existed for the NGOs to write their own parallel document. The UN had organized a parallel and even anticipatory NGO structure (with the NGOs meeting almost a full week before the governments in Durban), allowing the NGOs to have a significant voice, audience, and separate structure from which to try to influence the governmental declarations. These structures were mandated to develop a virtually finished draft document that could be amended and then ratified by the NGO Forum delegates. *Some* credit should be given to the UN High Commissioner for Human Rights, Mary Robinson, the ranking UN chair of WCAR. The UN structures created an organized forum for grassroots groups to challenge the world governments, literally handing the NGOs a golden opportunity. Caucuses and tendencies within the broad category of "NGO" had the chance to carry out militant challenges under UN auspices, and, at times, protections.

The question remained, who would, and could, provide leadership among the NGOs? Who could take advantage of those opportunities? As we will see, the sad answer was, "No one."

There are some NGOs, national and international, who make the UN a main site of their work, and have specific recognized status with the UN bodies called ECOSOC (Economic and Social Council) consultative status. These groups, e.g. Amnesty International, had some organizational authority to lead out of their experience in UN structures but did not reflect a multiracial base or a political point of view around which they had built support, either among the newer NGOs, or in actual communities, workplaces, or specific countries. Others, like SANGOCO (the South African NGOs Coordinating Organization) tried to call for plenary meetings but claimed they were overruled by the International Steering Committee. While these internal and factional conflicts are complex, one result of them was that these leadership structures were often invisible, and played no public role in trying, let alone succeeding, to organize, mobilize, and focus the activities of the many thousands of delegates who were new to UN proceedings—most of whom went there to *be* organized.

The logical site for such leadership would have been the opening plenary and yet the first day gave clear indications that no such structures of leadership or rank and file resistance existed. At first, watching 10,000 delegates fill a section of the stadium, with banners and chants from all over the world, there was a sense of hope. Within a few hours, however, it was clear that things didn't look good. This was not a serious political plenary but a bad attempt at a "feel good" diversion by the UN High Commission and the International Steering Committee; Scandinavian singing, African dancing, and militant but vague speeches masked a political crisis at the conference that was already in full swing.

What would have been reasonable and historically possible for new delegates to expect? *No leadership within NGO.*

We might have expected orientation to NGO and governmental structures, political leadership in analyzing the governmental document and preparing the NGO document, and tactical leadership on daily actions to impact media, the people of South Africa, and the governments. None of those took place.

Perhaps 90 percent or more of the NGO delegates had not attended any PrepComs for WCAR. That meant more than 9,000 people had come to Durban looking for direction and looking for structures in which to be effective. At a minimum, the opening NGO plenary could have provided some sense of structural, if not political, orientation. Instead, the canned opening show was a kickoff for a conference rife with backstage factional disputes among the NGO organizing committees, and within every NGO structure, including, unfortunately, many unresolved political conflicts among the South Africans themselves. Because Durban was the first UN meeting I had ever attended in my life, I had nothing to compare it to. But having subsequently attended three PrepComs for the forthcoming World Summit on Sustainable Development (WSSD) in Johannesburg (two at the UN Headquarters in New York and one in Bali, Indonesia), I have now seen far better structures for NGO leadership and participation. Such structures could have existed, and needed to exist, at WCAR.

For example, at WSSD there are two competing NGO leadership groups, the International Steering Committee (ISC), the official NGO steering committee authorized by the UN (which had a comparable structure at WCAR), and a relatively new structure, the Sustainable Development Issues Network (SDIN), an independently organized NGO caucus. Despite their competition and rancorous history, they both provide an important framework. They organize daily morning meetings at each PrepCom in which a general sense of orientation is provided. In that I spent most of my time at the SDIN meetings, the work of the Third World Network and several other NGO networks within those structures will be used as examples of what was needed and lacking at Durban.

Every day, at the Bali PrepCom for WSSD, held in May/June 2002, more than 150 of 500 NGO participants chose to attend the SDIN morning briefings. There they received an analysis of the governmental documents, reports on the fights among governments about policies and texts, and the suggested issues and language most possibly impacted by NGO pressure. It also provided a forum where NGO delegates trying to initiate daily actions could find a ready-made audience and could recruit to their specific tactical plans, with each delegate voting with her feet as to whether she agreed. At WCAR, although the governments were not yet meeting when the NGO conference began, there was a marked draft of the governmental document available to every delegate. Each section of the document was marked with bold letters and "brackets"; governments put language they were disputing in brackets, e.g. "[U.S. should take responsibility and pay reparations for the Trans-Atlantic Slave Trade]." Given that the NGOs had five days of preparation before the governments formally began their own sessions in Durban, it would have been possible to have a daily briefing on the governmental document, each day focusing on specific components that were weak or objectionable, led by representatives of NGOs that had taken leadership on those issues. Instead, there was *no* coordinated effort to publicly discuss the governmental document and to find ways to impact it. There were no daily meetings open to all NGO delegates for orientation or where debates about daily opportunities and tactical interventions could take place.

Ravi Nair, of the South East Asia Human Rights Network, whose organization independently put out a daily bulletin at WCAR, challenged the authority of those who had taken institutional power in the NGO structures preceding and during the conference:

> To begin with, the success of the conference depended upon the International Steering Committee (ISC) and the UN NGO Secretariat, represented by the regional NGOs. But in fact, the ISC and in most cases the regional NGOs had no moral authority to call a plenary, no moral authority to put forth any views on policy. Most of them are fly-by-night operators. If you had a ticket to Geneva you could play a role in the Preparatory Committees but these people had no constituency, no track record, and no outreach program. The only exception was the meeting of the Americas, held in Santiago, Chile, where many of the delegates had a certain legitimacy and generated substantive language that was not reflected in the final WCAR declarations.[9]

---

9. Ravi Nair, interview with the author, Durban, South Africa, 3 September 2001.

The Role of the Issue Caucuses

With no daily plenary at which a common program and tactical plan could be struggled out, the conference was set up so that if you wanted to be involved, you joined a specific workgroup or issue group. There were 39 such caucuses: Africa, South Africa, Africans and Afro-descendant, Americas, Caribbeans, HIV/AIDS, Women, Youth, Environmental Racism, Poverty and Racism, Indigenous peoples, Indigenous women, and so on. In terms of their impact on the overall WCAR processes, the issue caucuses reflected both the strengths and the weaknesses of the NGO forces and in no way could be called a NGO "movement." Given the power of Western imperialism and the growing disintegration of public life they so proudly call "civil society," it is often a good tactical approach that activists and organizers grab one piece of reality, one major problem that the system generates, and try to build an organization or even a cause around one specific and often profound abuse, such as global warming, police brutality against Black youth, educational racism, violence against women, or Third World debt. The list of good causes is almost infinite. Still, the challenge is how can we build a movement? How do we form a larger political organizations with a broader and more comprehensive political vision? How do we develop a totalizing strategy and organizing plan to challenge a totalizing enemy—in this case world imperialism led by the U.S?

Despite the dilemmas I discussed, the intention of the UN to divide people up to work on particular issues was actually a good idea. The general NGO document would gain its strength from the power and clarity of people working on the frontlines of actual struggles, who could bring an analytical focus to the actual language of the document, and from there, negotiate with the governments who generally want to weaken or delete the language. Moreover, many oppressed groups have needed specific organizational forms to advance their goals, often forming separate organizations to unify their own people. From there they can then address the specificity of their oppression as Indigenous peoples, Blacks, Latinos, Asian/Pacific Islanders, women, or Third World women. Each of these structures is in fact essential to the demands for self-determination, for sovereignty, and for finding ways to challenge the larger racist structures formed by Western imperialism.

In the specific political dynamics of Durban, no one was capable of organizing viable plenary sessions and no political leadership came forth to propose a program with lead demands, that could, in turn, provide context for the many particular demands. One example could have been that all the caucuses would prioritize support for the Palestinians, and for reparations, not at the expense of "their" issues, but in a way to express that the genocide against the Palestinian people and the crimes of the Trans-Atlantic Slave Trade are *all* of our issues. There were no open and effective left or organized groups trying, let alone succeeding, at such a tactical plan. In the absence of a more compelling overarching politics, the issue workshop structure fostered particularism and isolation. Each individual delegate or even small group of delegates had to make individual choices.

Again, without valorizing the subsequent World Summit on Sustainable Development, which has many distinct problems of its own, the model I hoped for in Durban *did* materialize at the Bali PrepCom for WSSD. It came in the form of an informal but functional left, feminist, Third World-centered, anti-corporate, anti-imperialist united front. At Bali, the existence of a daily structure for reports, announcements, and even the opportunity for NGOs to organize other NGOs, allowed a far greater opportunity for specific issue-based caucuses to find ways to focus on both the specificity of their central issue and, from that powerful base, to help generate and organize a common program more comprehensive and potent than the sum of its parts. At the Bali PrepCom, 13 NGO issue caucuses collaborated on an anti-U.S. demonstration, "What Are We Going to Do About The United States?" and organized against the idea of "public-private partnerships" being promoted by the U.S. to circumvent signed agreements among governments. We held a well-attended press conference denouncing the U.S. and G8 for imposing a corporate agenda on the conference, sabotaging progress on poverty reduction and on placing ecological constraints on the U.S. and EU production and consumption. The Women's Caucus in particular took tremendous leadership on many of those campaigns as did the Third World Network and Strategy Center.

It was this level of unified, creative daily tactics and coherent cooperation from issue-based NGOs that was missing at Durban and could have placed sustained pressure on the governments, whether or not the U.S. walked out. The excellent work in the individual, issue-based caucuses was later reflected in a strong NGO Forum Declaration, but even that was not more and in fact less than the sum of its parts. The caucus work did *not* translate into a vibrant conference-wide movement or a highly visible challenge to the world governments.

So What Were People Doing at WCAR?

If there were no daily orientation programs, no common actions to impact the delegates and no efforts at a common written program that could impact the governments, what exactly were people doing at Durban? What did the conference actually look like? Major Kobese, Program Coordinator of the South African NGO Coordinating Organization (SANGOCO), commenting on the second day of the conference, observed:

> There were no commissions yesterday. Today the delegates are wandering around aimlessly; the panels are in a mess; commissions have failed and will fail. The deadline for the submissions of the inputs is tomorrow. What will the nature of the final document be, considering that the thematic commissions will not have had any opportunity to provide substantive input? What will the final document out of this process represent, and whom? [10]

In the absence of structures for a real political convention, people created their own itineraries. Durban was organized like an antiracist fair with many organizations running booths to advertise their organization and their products in large tents around the Kingsmeade Cricket Stadium.

☐ There were daily issue caucus meetings in tents outside the stadium, in which 20 to 30 delegates fought over language on Dalits in India, Environmental Justice, Sex Trafficking, and Indigenous

---

10. "Program Coordinator of the NGO WCAR Secretariat calls for an NGO plenary," *Human Rights Features*, 30 August 2001, 1. (Exactly. The absence of NGO plenaries throughout WCAR, more than any internal struggles or factionalism, was the primary failing, because in such a public context, individual groups would have had the chance to vie for leadership and offer specific programs and proposals.)

peoples. Perhaps 1,000 people were directly involved in caucus writing and debates.

☐ Workshops organized general discussions of key issues, often, however, with no action plan to impact WCAR. Some NGOs had the objective of publicizing their work for an international audience, others of giving academic presentations to an international audience, and some of gaining international support for specific and popular antiracist struggles. While many of these were meritorious as workshops, others fell far short of what was historically required. Unfortunately, the efforts of organizations to publicize their own work did not evolve into a larger coordinated strategy.

☐ In some instances, there were large workshops of considerable import—historical inquiries into slavery and reparations, a panel of ten women from Indigenous peoples rights struggles, a chronicle of human rights abuses in Palestine, a compelling presentation about the struggle of Dalits—many with 500 or more attendees. These had the impact of popularizing a social movement, picking up international connections, and organizing the consciousness of other delegates.

☐ The South African Independent Media Center set up a media room with computers for NGO journalists, ran a website for the conference, and held daily press conferences, often well attended by NGO delegates. The press conference criticized Mbeki's opening speech to WCAR, publicized the demands of the Palestinians, and supported the Durban Social Forum coalition's critique of South African neoliberalism, in particular the privatization of public services such as water and its support for the demands of the landless movement.

☐ The African National Congress organized a well attended lecture series at the nearby University of South Africa (UNISA) campus at which speakers, including Blade Nzimande, General Secretary of the South African Communist Party, Jacob Zuma, Deputy President of South Africa, Aziz Pahad, Deputy Minister of Foreign Affairs, Mamoud Mamdani, a former Ugandan intellectual who is now a professor at Columbia University, Ibo Mandaza, a Zimbabwean Marxist political economist, and Samir Amin, an anti-imperialist author, modeled what a high level of principled political debate looked like.

☐ Many groups were able to set up meetings with South African intellectuals, organizers, and revolutionaries, ANC, SACP, and COSATU leaders, and those from the Durban Social Forum Coalition, or just approach them at the many public events in which they participated. Many U.S. NGOs who had worked in the anti-Apartheid struggle for years had built up many international contacts with South African leaders and were able to help facilitate meetings for other members of their delegations. For example, the Third World Women's Alliance and the Applied Research Center, both out of Oakland, California, organized large delegations of U.S. activists and set up tours of South African townships in Soweto and Alexandra and meetings with various left organizations in Durban, Capetown, and Johannesburg—many of whom were present at the Durban conference. Black Workers for Justice, based in Georgia and North Carolina, and the Environmental Justice Caucus also spent a great deal of time setting up meetings with their South African counterparts.

☐ The Palestinian NGOs generated public events everyday, spending most of their time out in the sunlight, away from the backroom word crafting. They held press conferences and organized daily traveling demonstrations of 50 to 100 people that went all over the Kingsmeade fairgrounds in search of audiences. They handed out leaflets, sought out Israeli delegates, who often sought them out as well, held angry public debates, and displayed large banners at the opening and closing plenary sessions: "Racism: Israelis Have Right To Return, Palestinians Do Not."

☐ The South African Congress of Trade Unions (COSATU) and the Durban Social Forum both organized large marches to protest specific policies of the South African government. These were profoundly important historical events but were also fundamentally internal to South African politics and the struggle of many forces to define the terms of self-determination. Neither focused on the United States as the main target, nor am I arguing that they should have. But for U.S. delegates trying to place the primary onus for racism on our own government and trying to make the strategic connection between racism and imperialism, these marches were no substitute for an independent tactical plan.

While all those events, especially taken as a whole, could easily provide a productive week in Durban, the challenge to the NGOs at the World Conference Against Racism was to make an international impact against racist policies and racist governments at Durban, in particular the United States and the G7. In that context, many of the events at WCAR, while of enormous educational value, did not serve those objectives.

The U.S. walk-out provided a ready-made vehicle for two days of protest. All NGO delegates could see a common enemy taking a bold and provocative step, and the world media in Durban saw the walk-out and the anti-U.S. NGO protests as "a good story." But had the U.S., instead, stayed in Durban and chosen to further impose its racist agenda on the entire conference through more formal UN structures, could the world NGOs have launched an effective confrontation? My sense is no. That would have required the completion of the NGO Forum Declaration with a well-publicized challenge to the governments as well as organized mass demonstrations against the U.S. for its failure to support true Palestinian self-determination, its failure to stop Israeli aggression and brutality, and its failure to support reparations. The U.S. walk-out offered an historical opportunity for a short-term resistance, which the NGOs carried out well. But as the NGO Forum limped into its last days, the very low level of organizational unity and capacity among at least 500 highly visible left antiracist activists in the U.S. delegation became more apparent. As such, while the heady events at Durban created a historical experience of a lifetime, they actually camouflaged an even greater crisis of will and organization among the NGOs and the absence of even the most minimally coordinated movement—even for the duration of WCAR alone.

The Challenge of Leadership in the World Antiracist Movement

In the specific context of Durban, the U.S. NGOs—given the prominent and destructive role played by the U.S. governmental delegation—were needed to play a prominent and constructive role in mobilizing a worldwide resistance to the U.S.

In particular, Black delegates from the U.S. have historically had the moral authority and legitimacy to lead the fight against slavery, apartheid in all its forms, genocide, and now reparations. Unfortunately, the conference also exposed profound splits and weaknesses within the Black Liberation Movement, and within the overall U.S. antiracist movement, that prevented such coordinated leadership.

In the absence of an organized antiracist movement, several forms of "legitimacy" are needed to be an effective leadership group: moral authority, political power, and organizational will and capacity. For example, the national March on Washington in 1963, a major antiracist united front, was led by what were called the "Big Five" civil rights groups—National Association for the Advancement of Colored People (NAACP), Urban League, Congress of Racial Equality (CORE), Southern Christian Leadership Conference (SCLC), and the Student Non-violent Coordinating Committee (SNCC). While they had enormous tensions among themselves, they were able to maintain a viable united front, at least for the duration of the march. The Kennedy Administration and the U.S. public *did* accept both their moral and political authority and the representative nature of the march that they called. The problem today, however, is not the political and strategic differences in the Black Liberation Movement, most of which would take years or decades to be resolved or even reduced, but the absence of the united front culture that characterized the movement in the 1960s. Such a renewed focus on the united front would give greater urgency to finding common plans of action, and creating some leadership and governance structures that could help resolve what seem to be historically endemic

lack of a united front

conflicts among particular individuals and groups that, at least so far, have proven intractable.

Unfortunately, no U.S. antiracist forces have anything near the moral authority that the frontline civil rights groups had in the 1960s. Jesse Jackson, who showed up in Durban surrounded, as usual, by a coterie of media, had more political authority than all the rest of the U.S. delegates combined. Despite the disagreements many of us have with Reverend Jackson for his binding ties to the Democratic Party and U.S. big business, his presence as a one-man movement was a walking criticism of the *lack of an organized antiracist united front in the U.S.* that was so needed at WCAR.

There was nothing, at least in theory, that would have prevented a U.S. coalition of antiracist forces from holding a pre-convention in the U.S. prior to WCAR. Such a conference could have elected representative leadership and agreed upon a common program and common tactical plan for WCAR. Such an antiracist convention could have had enormous capacity to impact every UN structure—the PrepComs, the regional meetings, the International Steering Committee, and the WCAR NGO delegates as well as setting up mass structures of participation at Durban.

Once in Durban, given the vacuum of official leadership at the UN NGO level and the enormous number of U.S. delegates (estimated at 3,000 or more out of a total of 10,000), any call for an open U.S. plenary meeting, to discuss draft program language and to lay out a tactical plan for the conference, could have drawn 1,000 delegates or more. But the problems would have been enormous and immediate. Who had the moral authority to call the meeting? Who had the political respect and trust of other delegates to put forth an initial political agenda, even for discussion? Which organizations would have had the unity, maturity, and capacity to withstand the inevitable attacks? And would there not have been a strong probability of the meeting breaking up into factional disputes? For all of those reasons, no forces even tried to organize such a meeting or to reach out to others to see if such an ambitious project were possible. In that individual South Africans and groups called for a *decision-making* NGO plenary but did not have the capacity or moral authority to make one happen, the dilemma was not particular to the U.S. delegation. There was a unique historical responsibility for the left antiracist forces in the U.S. to challenge our own government. In Durban, that coordinated campaign among U.S. NGOs was limited to the protest against the U.S. government walk-out. One objective of this strategic sum-up is to encourage a better outcome at the next international antiracist conference.

Drafting the NGO Forum Declaration and Programme of Action

The final WCAR NGO Forum Declaration sought to address many issues that would be relevant and historically essential in any comprehensive plan to reduce world racism. Yet, it was the product of an unrepresentative and flawed process whereby more than 90 percent of the NGO delegates played virtually no role in writing, discussing, or voting on it in any manner. The organizational amateurism and factionalism among the NGOs was very unfortunate, because the final document is quite impressive. It has compelling sections on reparations, Palestine,

environmental justice, and Dalits. In fact, many NGOs working on specific issues, e.g. immigration and women, look to
their own section of the document as a breakthrough for their
work. The problem is that the declaration was supposed to
be a highly publicized, historically on-time public document,
an actual tactic of intervention in an actual struggle. It failed
in that sense, in that most NGOs, even those who attended
Durban, have never seen or read it as it finally appeared long
after most of them left.

One dilemma that held up the NGO Declaration intermina-
bly was whether it was to be a "consensus document" in which
all parties had to agree with all sections, or a compilation of
each caucus's writings on each subject area. On September 3,
two days after the September 1 final plenary of the NGO Forum, 200 delegates (out of 10,000) were still arguing and
debating among themselves in an effort to finish the NGO Forum Declaration and Programme of Action.

At a press conference on September 3, several international
human rights organizations (Amnesty International, Human Rights
Watch, the International Service for Human Rights, the Lawyers
Committee for Human Rights, and Physicians for Human Rights)
tried to, in their words, "refocus" the NGO challenge to the governments in anticipation of their disagreements with the final
NGO Declaration. The groups' press conference was an effort,
in their view, to accomplish several things:

☐ They wanted to move the debate away from Palestine
and Israel and toward other key issues, such as "the
rights of Dalits and Roma, racial discrimination in criminal justice systems, the plight of extremely vulnerable

groups such as refugees, and dire health issues such as HIV/AIDS."[11]

☐ Some groups, such as the Lawyers Committee on Human Rights moved to distance themselves from what they felt was "inaccurate and inflammatory" language against Israel.

☐ Some wanted to criticize the decision to make the final document, not yet released, a "collection of voices from the victims" as opposed to a "consensus document" drafted to correspond to the specific language of the governmental document.

Many organizations and individuals at WCAR, including this author, fundamentally disagreed with all of their assumptions. First, who are these groups and who and what do they represent? There are too many groups, some with large staffs and big budgets, others with just a mailing list and post-office box, that try to project themselves as "international organizations" onto a world stage with no accountability to a grassroots base anywhere. At a conference in South Africa where the vast majority of delegates rallied behind the lead demands of reparations and Palestinian self-determination, who were these "human rights" groups to claim they represented the interests of Africans, Blacks, and Palestinians? None of them had a base in any of those oppressed constituencies. During the anti-U.S. protests, none of the "human rights" groups were present.

---

11. "Trying to Get Back on Track: Major international human rights organizations attempt to refocus meeting," *Human Rights Features*, 4 September 2001, 1.

Second, the criticism of the Palestinian and Arab caucuses
for "inaccurate and inflammatory" language against Israel at a
time of Israeli massacres of Palestinian civilians was, objectively,
a strong intervention on behalf of Israeli apartheid and racism.
The Palestinian people are fighting for their lives, having their land
stolen and their children murdered. What possible crime of inflammatory language could exist even in the same breath as the
inflammatory weapons the Israelis are using against Palestinian
civilians, in violation of every human rights statute in the world?
Even if some of the groups had specific tactical criticisms of the
Palestinian NGOs, the calling of a press conference to distance
yourself from Palestinian rhetoric is simply chauvinist. You don't
criticize the Vietnamese when they are having napalm dropped
on them by your own government. You don't criticize the Jews'
outcries when Hitler is putting them in the ovens. And you don't
criticize the Palestinians publicly for excessive language, unless you want to side with the United States and Israel, who
used that "language" as the pretext for their walk-out. This
language, by the way, after further investigation into the actual NGO text, proved to be analytical, factual, and consistent
with UN program protocols.

Third, generating a final NGO document based on negotiations between all the NGOs over each caucus' language, instead
of constructing a document based on the core contributions of
each caucus, is a recipe for disaster. Achieving "consensus language" would have involved all 39 different issue caucuses voting
on each section and each sentence of the final NGO Declaration and Programme of Action. Under this arrangement, the
Women's caucus would have veto power over language in the
Reparations section and the Dalit caucus would be debating the

declaration of the Palestine caucus until a "consensus" was reached. In that some NGOs felt they were mandated to mimic the UN government process of "consensus," it is no wonder that the document failed to meet its deadline.

With each caucus meeting often twice a day during Durban, there was the chance to hammer out consensus language within the *caucus*. At least in each issue caucus there was a chance for international unity, a chance for a coherent politics that could impact the governments and the world, a chance for a negotiated text, and the moral authority that the final language comes from participants with long track records on the issue in question.

Chee Yoke Ling, from the Third World Network in Malaysia, an experienced UN NGO leader who has spent the last ten years trying to build the NGO movement on issues of trade and the environment, raises real concerns about NGO efforts to draft broad manifestos parallel to those of the governments:

> Some of the NGOs are as bad as the governments. They behave in a self-important manner; they can never reach consensus or even simple agreements. I think the best way to reach greater agreements among NGOs is to begin with bilateral initiatives between specific groups with whom we have some political agreement and a history of common work. Then we generate a document and see who wants to sign onto it. If every group has editorial power we would have a movement of editors, not organizers.[12]

Building on this view, the NGO press conference at the WSSD PrepCom in Bali, Indonesia (a PrepCom for the 2002

---

12. Chee Yoke Ling, conversation with the author, New York, 28 January 2002.

WSSD) was a model of how this could have worked at Durban. In Bali, we organized a press conference of 13 different issue caucuses with each caucus focusing on its central issue. What did it come to Bali to achieve? Did it believe the governmental document reflected progress or regress on that issue? What was the caucus demanding? Unlike WCAR, the World Summit on Sustainable Development has no process for a parallel NGO document. One reason the press conference worked was because all of the caucuses had a *baseline political unity in theory and practice*—they saw transnational corporations and the United States sabotaging the work of the conference, and they had some actual practice together throughout two weeks of the PrepCom in preparing joint statements as well as organizing actual protests and demonstrations. Still, when those of us on the press conference planning group read each caucus's statement, we realized that each caucus did not really have complete agreement with each other caucus's statement (e.g. the Arab caucus's demand that world governments stop blockades against Iraq and Cuba). So, we came up with a format in which the spokespeople stated, "The Women's caucus says; the Energy caucus says, etc," with an understanding that each caucus spoke for itself and we did not speak for each other. And yet, that format, the "collection of voices of the victims" (versus "consensus" format) worked because none of us strongly wanted to disassociate ourselves from the views of any other caucus.

At WCAR, the strength of the final NGO Declaration was the passion and issue-specific knowledge of each section, written by each individual caucus. It was not, nor did it have to be, a "consensus" document. And the self-important human rights groups who felt embarrassed by the language of many of the caucuses, were in fact, inappropriately, trying to speak for the entire NGO Forum. Note that when they put forth *their* choice of critical issues, they completely omitted Palestinian self-determination (except to condemn its rhetorical excess) and reparations. That is, their effort to get the public message "back on track" came out of a "human rights bureaucracy" caucus no more representative, and in fact a great deal less so, than the African, Black, and Palestinian caucuses which gave the sharpest edge and the most profound content to the antiracist agenda.

I worry that it was the efforts of those who were arguing for a "consensus" document that may have been a major disruptive force, causing the document to never see the light of day while all the NGO delegates were still in Durban. The NGO Declaration never was available for a launch at the final plenary, never was printed in substantial quantities, and still, a year after WCAR, is not available as a mass produced document.

In retrospect, this was a lost opportunity. Had several of the key NGO caucuses been able to reach unity *with each other* instead of focusing on trying to cobble together the final declaration, the Indigenous peoples, Palestinian, African, Environmental Justice, and Reparations caucuses could have released their own language at a press conference. They could have supported each other's key demands, printed up an immediate document that was partial but in many ways more representative, and asked all the delegates at WCAR to rally around that document and bring its message to the governments. This could have had so much more impact than the fight for "consensus" on a parallel document that generated neither consensus nor a document that could impact WCAR.

The printed NGO Declaration finally arrived—days after the closing of the NGO Forum. Although the document has some impressive resolutions, it was never presented to an NGO plenary and was delivered to the public and the UN three days after almost all the NGO delegates left. Even when it was finally presented on September 4, only 15 copies were made available and even those had missing pages. In spite of this undesirable and ineffective process, the caucus model succeeded in generating a document worthy of study and use today.[13] This discussion is one such effort to continue its impact after the actual events in Durban.

A Textual Analysis of the Final NGO Declaration and Programme of Action

The final NGO Declaration contains important language on slavery, reparations, Israel, and Palestine. Many other important sections of the document—immigrants, women, Dalits, Roma, trafficking, in fact, all 39 issue caucuses—require study and commentary by activists in the field. I have chosen to focus on two key sections—Slavery/Reparations and Palestine/Israel, because those were the issues that most threatened the U.S., the issues over which the U.S. staged its walk-out, and in my view, the issues that represent key demands for a world antiracist Left. In this section, I compare the NGO language to the final governmental language on each subject and make some summary analytical conclusions.

---

13. "WCAR NGO Forum Declaration," 3 September 2001, <http://www.racism.org.za/declaration.htm> (31 July 2002).

Reparations for Africa, Blacks in the U.S., and the African Diaspora

Excerpts from the WCAR NGO Forum Declaration on Reparations

☐ "We recognize that the Trans-Atlantic Slave Trade and slavery, which constitute crimes against humanity, forced the brutal removal and the largest forced migration in history (over one hundred million), caused the death of millions of Africans, destroyed African civilizations, impoverished African economies and formed the basis for Africa's underdevelopment and marginalization which continues to this date. We acknowledge that Africa was dismembered and divided among European powers, which created Western monopolies for the continued exploitation of African natural resources for the benefit of Western economies and industries"(66).[14]

☐ "We strongly call on the UN to establish, within one year from this World Conference Against Racism, an international tribunal to measure the extent of the damages resulting from the slave trade, slavery, and colonialism on Africans and African Descendants. We call on the United Nations to establish and resource a world institute based in Africa and dedicated to research, fact finding, and resource networking for Africans and African Descendants in the Diaspora" (232).

☐ "We demand that the United States, Canada, and those European and Arab nations that participated in and benefited from the Trans-Atlantic Slave Trade, the Trans-Sahara Slave

---

14. Ibid., numbers in parentheses refer to the section numbers in the final WCAR NGO Forum Declaration.

Trade, the Trans-Indian Ocean Slave Trade, Slavery and the Colonization of Africa, within one year of the WCAR, to establish an international compensatory mechanism for victims of these crimes against humanity—reaching the masses of the victimized and not merely an elite few..." (237, 240).

□ "[We demand] restitution encompassing the unconditional return of land, heritage icons and artifacts; the provision of land to those forced to leave their homelands and forcibly resettled in foreign lands; cancellation of debt of countries victimized by these crimes against humanity including African countries and impoverished countries in the Americas" (241).

□ "[We demand] monetary compensation that will repair the victims... programs for the creation and enhancement of participation in production enterprises; full accessibility and affirmative inclusion in all levels of employment opportunity; grants of cash payments based on assessment of losses resulting from the violation of human rights and crimes against humanity" (242).

□ "[We demand] restoration including release of all political prisoners, providing for health care, including mental health care, educational and social services that are specifically designed to correct the injuries caused by the violations of human rights and crimes against humanity" (243).

□ "[We demand] Satisfaction and guarantee of non-repetition includes the public acknowledgment of the crimes against humanity, the correction of the history of Africa,

African and African descendants in educational materials, in the media, acknowledgments of the economic base of exploitation of the victims…and the unjust enrichment of the perpetrators" (244).

☐ "We call for an independent international and regional monitoring organization with the responsibility to assure that programs of reparations are designed and implemented with timetables that satisfy the provision of this program of action is accomplished" (245).

☐ "We call on all concerned African nations to take formal action to obtain the return of stolen cultural artifacts, gold, money, mineral wealth and the return of the occupied land on the continent and call on the international community to support such actions" (247).

Excerpts from the UN Governmental WCAR Declaration on Reparations

☐ "We acknowledge that slavery and the slave trade, including the Trans-Atlantic Slave Trade, were appalling tragedies in the history of humanity not only because of their abhorrent barbarism but also in terms of their magnitude, organized nature and especially their negation of the essence of the victims and further acknowledge that *slavery and the slave trade were crimes against humanity* [author's italics] and are among the major manifestations of racism, racial discrimination, xenophobia, and related intolerance, and that Africans and peoples of African descent, Asians and peoples of Asian descent, and indigenous peoples were vic-

tims of these acts and continue to be victims of their consequences" (13).[15]

☐ "We acknowledge and profoundly regret the massive human sufferings and the tragic plight of millions of men, women,
and children caused by slavery, slave trade, Trans-Atlantic
Slave Trade, apartheid, colonialism and genocide, and call
upon states concerned to honor the memory of victims of past
tragedies. We affirm that wherever and whenever these occurred they must be condemned and their re-occurrence
prevented..."(99).

☐ "We further note that some States have taken the initiative
to apologize and have paid reparations where appropriate, for
grave and massive violations committed" (100).

☐ "We recognize the efforts of developing countries, in particular the commitment and the dedication of African leaders
to seriously address the challenges of poverty, underdevelopment, marginalization, social exclusion, economic
disparities, instability, and insecurity, through initiatives such
as the New Africa Initiative and other mechanisms such as
the World Solidarity Fund for the Eradication of Poverty and
call upon developing countries, the United Nations, and its
Specialized Agencies, as well as international financial institutions to provide... new and additional financial resources
as appropriate to support these initiatives" (157).

---

15. United Nation General Assembly, "Programme of Action," *Report of the World
Conference Against Racism, Racial Discrimination, Xenophobia, and Related
Intolrance*, A/CONF.189/12, 25 January 2002.

☐ The governmental document then laid out a long list of remedies to address African "poverty, marginalization, social exclusion, economic disparities, instability, and insecurity" including "debt relief, poverty eradication, building or strengthening democratic institutions, promotion of foreign direct investment, market access, transfer of technology, education, training and cultural development, mutual assistance in the reparation of illegally obtained and illegally transferred (stashed) funds in accordance with national and international instruments, restitution of art objects, historical artifacts, and documents to their country of origin in accordance with bilateral agreements or international instruments" (158).

The Politics of Reparations—A Short-term Victory with Danger Signs Emerging

The NGO resolutions reflect a major breakthrough in content, regardless of the many contradictions within the African states and the Black Liberation Movement in the U.S. In terms of its polemical and strategic approach, the NGO Declaration addresses many potential pitfalls in, and attacks upon, the nascent Reparations Movement:

☐ It offers structural and systematic demands that would take centuries to implement, and would preclude efforts by the West to "settle all claims."

☐ Its proposal that the West admit to crimes against humanity and institute a cultural introspection to acknowledge that it was built on the Trans-Atlantic Slave Trade would, of course, put the West on the moral, political, and legal defensive.

If West admits to crimes associated w/ the Trans Atlantic Slave Trade, they would be on the defensive side

☐ It included, but did not restrict reparations to, individual monetary compensation. It addressed the complexity of the return of land, cancellation (not "relief") of debt, return of art and artifacts, massive expansion of foreign payments for social services, including mental health care for the ongoing pain of colonialism, release of political prisoners, and the correction of the historical record through the creation of tribunals and research institutions. That is, it addressed a comprehensive cultural, economic, structural, psychological payback that involves a complete turning of the tables with the West.

The governmental declaration is complex. On the one hand, it provides language that for the first time admits that slavery was a "crime against humanity," a major breakthrough of the work of the Reparations Movement that may open the door to future legal claims in both national and international courts. Several governmental delegates from the EU told me that the language was carefully drawn, in order to get European and U.S. support, to make a heartfelt apology but to preclude any legal liability. Obviously, for most in the Reparations Movement, there can be no "heartfelt" anything without opening the door to legally enforceable reparations. Still, other legal scholars, such as Charles Ogletree, co-chair of the Reparations Coordinating Committee, argue that this is a major legal breakthrough for the Reparations Movement, in that "crimes against humanity" is a specific legal concept in international law that can contribute to both liability and remedy.[16] Much of this will be

---

16. Charles Ogletree, "Litigating the Legacy of Slavery," *New York Times*, 31 March 2002.

tested in future reparations litigation, but as a first step, this was an important victory that should be given even greater attention and scrutiny.

Having admitted that slavery was a "crime against humanity," there is no offer of reparations in the final UN governmental document, as the text makes clear, by the perpetrators of the Trans-Atlantic, Trans-Sahara, or Trans-Indian Ocean Slave Trade. There is no support for the institutional structures proposed by the NGO declaration to study and document the impacts and scope of slavery, and no willingness whatsoever to address the issue of reparations squarely, except to say that some unnamed nations have already granted reparations.

Worse, after the vaguely-worded general sentiments of apology, the governmental document takes a dangerous U-turn—trying to substitute a U.S./G8 imposed "free market" diet of "aid" and "economic development" for reparations—that steers clear of the demands for reparations. Unfortunately, while the Mbeki tendency within the ANC government has played an active role in the UN governmental policy debate on reparations, it has equated its immediate demand for "economic development aid" from the West *with its definition of reparations*. This is in sharp disagreement with the political, moral, ideological, historical, analytical, and strategic approach reflected in the NGO Declaration.

The problem with situating the demand for reparations into more immediate, state-to-state demands for "ensuring equitable market access and fair competition," "bridging the digital divide" and "democratizing international institutions such as the IMF, World Bank, and WTO" is that they, in fact, undercut the Reparations Movement by:

☐ Eliminating the entire process of documenting the crimes of slavery;

☐ Reducing a mass question of individual and group rights to a state-to-state negotiation, replacing direct democracy with "representative democracy;"

☐ Reducing a cultural, ideological, and political campaign that must take centuries, to a series of very immediate efforts to reduce the profound vulnerability of the African governments in a world market that is a stacked deck.

reparations (problem)

Many of the West's aid proposals mirror a neoliberal development model. There is the danger that the West will make tiny concessions to African states in return for luring them even further into a globally integrated imperialist system dominated by the United States and the EU—a system that will even further strengthen the ropes of dependency.

But it should be agreed upon that such programs have nothing whatsoever to do with reparations and should not be used by either the slave-trading West or the African nations fighting for self-determination, as a substitute, in any way, for a Reparations Movement. The ANC leadership has enormous moral authority in the world. Whatever plans and strategies it has for South Africa's development, it should be careful to not give the impression that its proposals for Western investment in any way compete with or undermine the fledgling Reparations Movement.

There is the view within the nascent Reparations Movement, with which I am allied, that no government and no civil rights or antiracist group or coalition is authorized to "sign off" or "settle" the demand for reparations. According to this view, each generation, in each nation, has the right to evolve its own understanding of specific remedies and demands (which in itself will involve the most contentious arguments) but no generation has the right to play into the hands of Western bourgeois law in which the entire purpose of "settlement" is to indemnify the perpetrators from any future claims against them and to settle "all present and future claims." No generation can settle all claims for future generations.

Within the Global South, there is a raging debate about how to effectively and democratically exercise state power, how to drive out, or at least limit, colonial economic penetration, and how to win true self-determination. These ideas were once at the center of anti-imperialist movements in the Third World. Now, governments and anti-imperialist movements in the Global South are fighting to re-establish their authority and viability in the present reactionary climate. At Durban, we saw the power of the structural demands for reparations and its enormous threat to the ideological and cultural hegemony of Western imperialism. The struggle for reparations will be central to the rebuilding of a Black Liberation Movement and a multiracial left antiracist movement in the U.S. and throughout Africa. It can provide a framework for a programmatic center of a Black and African renaissance that can impact and reshape a world Left and have profound impacts in Africa, Asia, Latin America, and among oppressed nationality peoples all over the world, including those in the United States. Given its profound potential and relatively fragile organizational state at present, the Reparations Movement and its future evolution must be carefully protected and supported.

Palestine—Who Was Hijacked?

The Palestinian people have been subjected to the most unprincipled and racist attacks as they struggle to restore their own nation, their own territorial integrity, and their own political and cultural identity in the face of an international campaign of slander and distortion. At Durban, the primary objectives of the Palestinian movement were to popularize their cause in front of an international audience, to articulate their demands to buttress the concept of Palestinian self-determination, and to stop the Israeli aggression against the Palestinian people, the military occupation of their land, and U.S. support for it. In that the NGO Forum Declaration was an ideological document, the Palestinian NGO delegates' goals were to win an international vote of confidence in their movement and an international condemnation of Israel's policies to help move forward an eventual political solution on terms favorable to the Palestinians.

These were life and death objectives. The Palestinians hoped to win a moral victory, to stay the hand of Israeli violence and conquest, to challenge the Israeli assassination of leaders and murdering of civilians, to stop the illegal occupations by Israeli settlers, and to cut off U.S. military and economic aid to Israel of more than $5 billion a year that pays for and encourages these abuses. The Palestinian delegates at WCAR worked to back up their charges against the Israelis of "racism," "apartheid," and "genocide." This was an effort to win the battle of ideas and to confront the way that Israel has manipulated the deserved worldwide sympathy for the Jews because of the horrors of the Holocaust carried out by the Germans, Italians, Poles, Austrians, and French, and tried to turn it into support for, or silence on, the terror that the Israelis are imposing on the Palestinians.[17]

Excerpts from the WCAR NGO Forum Declaration on Palestine

☐ "Affirming the right of the Palestinian people to self-determination, statehood, and independence and freedom, and the right of the return as stipulated in UN Resolution 194" (20).

☐ "The Palestinian people... are currently enduring a colonialist, discriminatory military occupation that violates their fundamental human right to self-determination including the illegal transfer of Israeli citizens into the occupied territories and establishment of a permanent illegal Israeli infrastructure; and other racist methods amounting to Israel's

---

17. The use of any analogies with Nazi Germany to describe Israeli treatment of the Palestinians should be done with the greatest of care; there are many abuses in the world that need not invoke Nazi war crimes. But especially after the latest round of efforts by the Sharon government to literally "wipe out" the Palestinian resistance, the dividing up of all Palestinian land into cantons, the military re-occupation of refugee camps, the use of "shoot to kill" orders indiscriminately, the assassination of Palestinian leaders and the holding hostage of their acknowledged president Arafat, even many former close allies of the Israeli people such as Desmond Tutu, and a growing number of courageous Israeli intellectuals such as Yitzhak Laor are choosing to make analogies with Hitler in a way to signal to the Israeli government that any last honeymoon or pulling of punches is over. Laor writes, "Amir Oren, a senior military commentator for Ha'aretz, quoted a senior military officer, 'In order to prepare properly for the next campaign, one of the Israeli officers in the territories said that it is justified and in fact essential to learn from every possible source. If the mission is to seize a densely populated refugee camp, or take over the kasbah of Nablus, and if the commander's obligation is to try to execute the mission without casualties on either side, then he must first analyze and internalize the lessons of earlier battles—even, however shocking it may sound, even how the German army fought in the Warsaw Ghetto.'" Yitzhak Laor, "After Jenin," *London Review of Books* 24, no. 9 (2002).

brand of apartheid and other racist crimes against humanity. Recognizing therefore that the Palestinian people have the clear right under international law to resist such occupation by any means provided under international law until they achieve their fundamental human right to self-determination and end the Israeli racist system" (98).

□ "Appalled by the on-going colonial military Israeli occupation of the Occupied Palestinian Territories (the West Bank including Jerusalem, and the Gaza Strip), we declare and call for an immediate end to the Israeli systematic perpetration of racist crimes, including war crimes, acts of genocide and ethnic cleansing (as defined in the Statute of the International Criminal Court) including uprooting by military attack, imposition of measures... on the population to make life so difficult that the only option is to leave the area, and state terrorism against the Palestinian people. Recognizing that all of these methods are designed to ensure the continuation of an exclusively Jewish state with a Jewish majority and the expansion of its borders to gain more land, driving out the indigenous Palestinian population" (160).

□ "We declare Israel is a racist, apartheid state in which Israel's brand of apartheid as a crime against humanity has been characterized by separation and segregation, dispossession, restricted land access, denationalization, 'bantustanization' and inhumane acts" (162).

□ "We recognize that targeted victims of Israel's brand of apartheid and ethnic cleansing methods have been in particular children, women, and refugees, and condemn the disproportionate numbers of children and women killed and injured in military shooting and bombing attacks" (164).

☐ "[We are] appalled by the discrimination against the Palestinians inside Israel which include: the imposition of discriminatory laws, including discriminatory laws of return and citizenship, which emphasize the ethnicity of the Israeli state as a Jewish state; the granting of benefits or privileges solely to Jewish Israeli citizens, the imposition of restrictions on the civil and political rights of Palestinians because of their national belonging or because they do not belong to the majority ethnic group; the negation of the right of Palestinians to equal access to resources of the State and civil equality, including affirmative action policies, which recognize the historical discrimination against Palestinians inside Israel" (165).

Excerpt from the UN Governmental WCAR Response on Palestine

The world governments rejected this language and passed a far more conciliatory position that, in essence, represented a victory for the U.S. and Israeli line on the subject:

"We are concerned about the plight of the Palestinian people under foreign occupation. We recognize the inalienable right of the Palestinian people to self-determination and to the establishment of an independent state and we recognize the right to security for all states in the region, including Israel, and call upon all states to support the peace process and bring it to an early conclusion" (60).

The language of the UN governments included no criticisms whatsoever of Israeli racism, brutality, or apartheid. This was hardly surprising given the strength of the U.S. and Israel and the weakness, internationally, of the Palestinians, and given the capitulation of most of the Arab states, many of whom have neocolonial dictatorial regimes closely allied with and dependent upon the U.S. The general statements in support of a Palestinian "independent state" are meaningless. Such statements are not even buttressed by specific reference to far stronger UN resolutions on Palestine already passed, in particular UN Resolution 194 which grants Palestinian refugees the right of return to their homes of origin, and UN Resolutions 242 and 338 which call for the immediate end to Israel's illegal occupation of the West Bank and Gaza Strip.

Nonetheless, the expansion of support for the Palestinian movement cannot be understood by the cold, harsh words of the WCAR governmental document. After all, if it was such a victory for the U.S. and Israel, why did the U.S. need to walk out?

A big part of the Palestinian organizing work is to create an ideological counteroffensive, to beat back the onslaught of unprincipled attacks from U.S., Israeli and Zionist ideologues, amplified by a pro-Israeli world press, that have kept their movement so often on the defensive. At the UNISA debates, Blade Nzimande, Secretary General of the South African Communist Party asked, "Why is there not more outrage about the mass murders of the Palestinians? I do not use this word lightly, but is this not genocide? How can we build more support for their struggle?"[18]

---

18. Blade Nzimande, author's notes, ANC lecture series at UNISA, 1 September 2002.

On the first day of WCAR, right after the opening plenary, the South African Independent Media Center held a press conference in which South African Leftists affiliated with the Durban Social Forum raised criticisms of Thabo Mbeki's just-concluded opening speech to the NGO delegates. During the questions and answers, seemingly out of the blue, a European NGO delegate asked the panelists, "Don't you think the Palestinian charges of racism and apartheid against Israel are deflecting from the other key antiracist issues we are trying to raise here?" Oupa Lehulere, from Khanya College in Johannesburg, replied, "That was the same criticism some people raised about the anti-Apartheid struggle for decades, that somehow our struggle against Apartheid was 'crowding out' other causes. We thought that the struggle against the Apartheid regime was in fact giving a focus to an international antiracist movement. Today, the Palestinian struggle is on the frontlines. They are risking their lives every day. They inspire people all over the world. If the Palestinians win, we all win."[19] While his remarks carried the day, the criticism of the Palestinians for being too militant, or organizing too well, at a time when their entire movement and story is being suppressed, reflects what some have called "soft Zionism" and perhaps anti-Arab racism even within the world antiracist movement that requires constant struggle and vigilance.

Later, during the heated debates among U.S. NGOs about the best politics and tactics to protest the U.S. governmental walk-out, a few Black civil rights moderates argued that the Palestinians "provoked" the U.S. and Israel to leave. Then, a few

---

19. Oupa Lehulere, statement at press conference, South African Independent Media Center, 27 August 2001.

Black delegates who had been working on the reparations issue, who did not buy the "provocation" argument, still proposed that any statements criticizing the U.S. walk-out should be restricted to the demands for reparations. They argued that the Palestinian issue was distracting from media coverage of the crimes of the Trans-Atlantic Slave Trade and preventing progress on the issues of reparations. As reported earlier, each time that these critiques were raised, the vast majority of U.S. Black delegates and NGO delegates of all races backed the Palestinian cause as well. As several of us argued, if you read the language of the NGO Declaration on reparations, even the most minimal interpretation of those demands essentially asks the U.S. and the European states to commit political suicide. Do we really expect the U.S. and the Europeans, who have committed mass murder systematically and structurally from their inception, to agree to the formation of, let alone abide by the recommendations of, a world court on reparations? Do we understand that even the most minimal but substantial economic payback for slavery to Blacks in the U.S., Africa, and the African Diaspora would virtually bankrupt the U.S.? Again, what have the oppressed and politically isolated Palestinian people done but try—with sticks and stones, bare fists, and, if necessary, their lives—to fight for their survival, and how can that not enormously help the movement for reparations? In that context, what in the world do the Palestinians have to do with this problem of Western arrogance and racism? Is their struggle a cause, or a symptom? And do we think, even for a nanosecond, that the U.S., able to bomb entire societies with impunity, walked out over "language" from the Palestinians, or "resolutions" from WCAR?

Then there are charges by pro-Israeli U.S. Jews and Israelis that they were harassed, even attacked verbally by the Palestinians at Durban and subjected to anti-Semitic slanders. They argue that the Palestinians provoked fights with the Israeli delegates, and that, of course, the U.S. walked out to protect the "human rights" of the Israeli delegates from Palestinian attacks. This is just not true. I was at Durban for two weeks, attended every plenary session, walked around Kingsmeade every day, and talked to the Palestinian delegates several times. Even given my support for the Palestinians, if I had seen what I felt were anti-Semitic attacks on Jewish and Israeli delegates, I would have stood up against them. At one time I saw a Palestinian demonstration and a bitter argument between Palestinian and Israeli delegates. I should hope there would be bitter argument as the Israelis are killing the Palestinians as a people. Still, the myth of physical attacks on Israeli or Jewish delegates is typical misinformation—the Palestinians were doing their job fighting for their lives, and given the deaths of their children, they were amazingly restrained and diplomatic. This despite the Israeli army's newfound penchant for painting the Star of David on Palestinian buildings and homes. Moreover, since the Israelis have tried to slander Jewish opponents of their brutality as "self-hating Jews," I suppose they would not be dissuaded from their cries of anti-Semitism to learn that when some Jewish WCAR delegates approached the Palestinian protestors as Jews to offer their sympathy and solidarity, we were literally embraced physically and emotionally, in a bear hug of internationalism.

Six months later I met an Israeli delegate to the World Summit on Sustainable Development at the UN in New York. She certainly felt enough ambivalence about Israeli policy to confide in me that a few of her friends are beginning to lose faith in the whole Zionist idea—still, she was more upset by Palestinian counter-violence than by that of her own government. She repeated to me the story that was going all over Israel that the U.S. walked out to prevent the Israelis from verbal and physical abuse. I tried to reason with her. Would we criticize the Vietnamese for screaming at U.S. supporters of the war in Vietnam? Is screaming and yelling "abuse," or in this case, making a desperate cry for help and support, totally appropriate behavior? Were the Israelis really in any danger at WCAR, even with their government's mass murder of Palestinian civilians? What exactly is polite and diplomatic behavior in the midst of genocide? As I described objectively what had happened, she said, "You should tell that story to others. On this one I feel our government has deceived us about Durban."[20]

In April 2002, the Israeli army initiated the Jenin massacre— another war crime initiated by Israeli Prime Minister Ariel Sharon, who many in the world call the "butcher" for his role in the earlier massacre of Palestinian civilians at the Sabra and Shatila refugee camps in South Lebanon in 1982. As with many of the world's abuses today, one can only wonder how the Palestinian people continue their fight for liberation and how those of us appalled at Israeli brutality can land effective blows.

The story of the Palestinian resistance at Durban and the WCAR NGO resolutions in which the Palestinians documented specific abuses and violations of international law are positive examples of what advance planning for such a conference can achieve.

---

20. Israeli NGO delegate to WSSD PrepCom II, conversation with the author, United Nations, New York, 5 February 2002.

I am convinced the Palestinians made new and stronger allies in the U.S., and throughout the world. The growing international outcry against Israeli policies, including a growing militancy among Israeli army reserve "refuseniks," the open analogy between Israeli behavior and Nazi tactics by both Israeli supporters and opponents of the attacks on Palestinian refugees, and the recent international appeal for support for the Palestinians by former South African Archbishop Desmond Tutu continue the positive legacy of WCAR.[21]

The Final Plenary: Running on Empty

Six days after it began, the NGO Forum at WCAR held its closing plenary session. It turned out to be the mirror image of the opening plenary—two book-ends with no book inside. As the WCAR meeting of the world governments had already started, this was the last chance for the NGOs to raise a coherent, organized political challenge to the world's governments. It didn't happen.

On Saturday, September 1st, as the NGO delegates once again returned to Kingsmeade Cricket Stadium for the closing plenary of the NGO Forum, there was a long delay in the beginning of the program. There was a growing buzz, "What is going on?" "What is the program?" "Where is the political declaration?" Soon, this implied critique of the leadership was drowned out by a far louder buzz, "I hear that Fidel is coming, Fidel is coming!" Soon, an advance guard of Cuban organizers began distributing paper Cuban flags. People were literally stepping over each other to get them, a combination of revolutionary sentiment

21. Desmond Tutu, "Apartheid in the Holy Land," *The Guardian*, 29 April 2002.

and a pent up desire to do something. Then, after perhaps an hour of anticipatory chanting—for Fidel, for the Palestinians, for ourselves—a ten car caravan arrived. Fidel Castro Ruiz, the president of Cuba, stepped out and was received like a revolutionary rock star. Except for the COSATU and Durban Social Forum demonstrations, each outside of the aegis of the WCAR, this was the first time during the conference that people had anything about which to be militant, antiracist, and, yes, anti-imperialist. Even though many of the delegates from the U.S. and Third World NGOs had positioned themselves as moderate, some even explicitly anti-revolutionary, it was as if Fidel Castro—the man who stood up to the giant, the U.S.—represented everyone's most revolutionary sentiments.

At the NGO plenary, Fidel spoke for two hours. And while he has not lost his profound ability to agitate, he is equally skilled as a propagandist in bringing complex ideas to an advanced audience. His major theme was the relationship of racism to imperialism, and the truly desperate condition of the Third World today under the domination of the United States, the "unchallenged superpower." Here is a head of state from a tiny island that had been ravaged by the slave trade, subject to Spanish and then U.S. colonialism, subjected to the classical tyranny of United Fruit Company and the U.S. Mafia and now, with no military or economic aid from a Soviet Union that no longer exists, he is still willing to openly challenge U.S. imperialism—morally, politically, and intellectually, in a world arena. In that brief historical moment, the power of an anti-imperialist socialism and just the simple courage of a leader and a nation willing to stand up to the world's bully gave Fidel the real mantle of the "leader of the free world."

Even though most delegates were thrilled to hear Fidel Castro, under the actual time, place, and conditions of WCAR, Fidel's speech was not an appropriate use of two hours of the final session. This was the last chance for the presentation of the NGO Declaration Programme of Action. It was the final debate and the final effort to mobilize the delegates, if only to ratify a declaration most of them had never seen, and to develop a plan to use that document to impact UN governmental policy in the world fight against racism. Instead, the UN NGO bureaucracy, by featuring the West's anathema, Fidel Castro, as the final and featured speaker at the WCAR NGO Forum, created a distraction as a cover for their own failures. Had there been a viable tactical plan to produce and distribute the Declaration presented to the NGO delegates, had their been even a hint of a grassroots NGO movement at Durban, Fidel could have been a great addition for emphasis. But Fidel is no substitute for the absence of an international movement or a viable conference. As thousands of WCAR delegates filed out of the stadium, they went home in much the same state as they had arrived—dedicated and angry, but fundamentally isolated, alienated, and disorganized. While it would have been naïve to expect a week in Durban to change those conditions, the World Conference Against Racism reflected the organizational and political disunity in the world antiracist movement more than it was able to remedy it, or even move the process forward. It would take those who were there, who saw the opportunity and the enemy in front of their own eyes, to pick up the pieces and reconstruct a new image and a new reality out of the many fragments and jewels that WCAR did produce.

A Sum-Up of WCAR's Historical Contributions

How does one understand the historical impact of an event like the World Conference Against Racism? Even before the massive post-September 11 backlash, Durban did not create the world challenge to the U.S. that it so richly deserved. The U.S. in general and the Bush Administration in particular had already calculated the cost of walking out, after barely walking in. The Republican Right hardly had to worry about the most radical and militant world forces or about a small sector of angry Black community activists, in that it already writes off more than 90 percent of the Black vote. Many of the weaknesses of WCAR were the limits of the historical period and the historical balance of forces in which it took place. With all the many limitations and indeed failures that I have tried to analyze squarely, there were some important components of the event that warrant final comment, some of which offer hopeful possibilities for future organizing work.

WCAR Exposed the Achilles Heel of the United States, Despite Its Enormous World Power

Generally, the United States forces others to walk out of international meetings as it controls the rules of the game at the UN, at the World Trade Organization, and in virtually every arena in which it operates. So why has the U.S. boycotted the two previous UN conferences against racism and used the flimsy pretext of Israel to hide its own vulnerability at WCAR? Why is the U.S. so afraid of a world debate on racism? Because racism has been the ideology, not of "discrimination" alone, but of the far more fundamental crimes upon which U.S. society has been built: slavery and genocide. Antiracism, when tied to anti-imperialist movements and strategy, contains the seeds of a revolutionary challenge to the existing order. There is encouragement to be found in the U.S. over-reaction, or perhaps appropriate reaction, to the challenges of an antiracist movement. In Europe as well, other Western capitalists are demonstrating their own vulnerability on the issue of racism as it relates to reparations. France passed a law in 2001 that "recognized the Trans-Atlantic Slave Trade as well as the slave trade across the Indian Ocean" as "crimes against humanity." This contradicted the European Union's public stance which has, so far, refused to make such an acknowledgment. While many Africans in French speaking former colonies praised France's leadership, France went out of its way at a press conference at WCAR to distinguish between slavery and colonialism. To some this may seem like a distinction without a difference, but it has profound political and legal ramifications. Politically, it seems to be saying that "colonialism," the foundation upon which every European nation and the U.S. has been built, is not in itself a "crime against humanity" whereas the slave trade is a "crime against humanity," a difference between what France is and what France did—a distinction that really can't be made. But also, as explained to me by several African delegates to WCAR, in their view the French government was trying to make a substantial apology for its past actions while simultaneously trying to protect itself from legal claims in a world court. Many European governments want to negotiate an "apology" as a way of "settling all claims" which the worldwide Reparations Movement would never accept. The point is that slavery, colonialism, and the demand for reparations are intertwined, and at Durban we saw the G8 powers, at least for a moment, on the defensive in the face of an antiracist offensive. The strategic lessons must be fully understood and applied in the most rigorous and militant manner to present conditions.

The Reparations Movement is Happening— There is No Going Back

At Durban, we saw not just the strategic weakness of the U.S. and European nations on racism but their literal panic in the face of demands for reparations. The U.S. in particular understands the scope of the programmatic demands of a Reparations Movement. Moreover, the U.S., as distinct from the European states, has a Black population of more than 34 million people located in every strategic urban center—New York, Washington D.C., Philadelphia, New Orleans, Atlanta, Houston, Detroit, Chicago, Oakland/San Francisco, and Los Angeles. If we carefully review the NGO declaration on slavery and reparations previously described in this chapter, we will understand that the many components of redress and restitution—punishment for the perpetrators, making the victims whole—will involve demands that are so revolutionary they can barely be imagined—just as the depravity of each individual European and white U.S. colonist and slaveholder murdering each of the tens of millions of individual Africans and Indigenous peoples can barely be imagined.

The Reparations Movement has the opportunity to create the central defining political framework for Black and left politics in the U.S. in the 21st century. It can become the most historical, ideological, and material challenge to Western imperialism and can frame a new series of initiatives among Blacks, Latinos, Asian/Pacific Islanders, Indigenous peoples, and antiracist whites to reconstruct new politics and new organizational forms for the antiracist movement. It can build new bridges between Blacks in the U.S. and African nations, provide a broader base of support for the urgent demands of 400,000 Indigenous peoples throughout the world, and put the system back on the political defensive.

The United Nations: Site for Anti-Imperialist Movement Building

While Malcolm X (and W.E.B. DuBois and Paul Robeson before him) used the United Nations as an important tactic in the struggle for Black liberation in the U.S., many grassroots activists, for good reason, are skeptical. The United Nations is still an institution headquartered in and dominated by the United States. The U.S. has always threatened and bullied the UN, withholding its dues as ransom against policies with which it disagrees and maintaining a completely selective and arbitrary posture toward UN resolutions. The U.S. shoves resolutions down the throats of nations when it serves its interests but blatantly refuses to abide by any resolutions that it sees as limiting its national sovereignty. Thus, UN votes are the ultimate stacked deck.

The recent actions by the U.S. in the UN Security Council to defy the authority of the International Criminal Court (ICC) raise imperial arrogance to legendary levels. The nations of the world ratified the ICC, and the Security Council, always dominated by the U.S., voted to require all governments involved in UN "peacekeeping missions" to abide by its provisions, in particular that any troops committing war crimes under UN auspices would be prosecuted under the ICC. It provides a reasonable reassurance to nations inviting in UN troops that troops will not torture, rape, or murder civilians or prisoners of war. The U.S.

threatened England, Mexico, and other Security Council members that if they did not grant U.S. troops an exemption from the ICC, the U.S. would not participate in any peace keeping missions. The Security Council members should have let the U.S. go, leaving the U.S. as a pariah on human rights. Instead, the U.S. twisted one arm after another; the Security Council reversed its original motion and agreed by a 15-0 vote to exempt the U.S. from the International Criminal Court's authority for one year, with a series of renewable one year exemptions obtainable until infinity. This incident brought disgrace and humiliation upon every member of the Security Council and the UN as an institution, but again, that was the U.S. strategy—to show time and time again that it is the world's policeman and will not be restrained by any principles or any collective institutions. This goes beyond hubris; it's a calculated strategy to terrorize the world.

Knowing this, why would antiracist forces, environmental and human rights forces, Indigenous peoples, anti-imperialist forces, or any progressive people waste their time at the UN? Because, with all its dilemmas, it is not a waste of time; it is a critical site of international struggle at this point in history.

Given the weak state of the international movement, the United Nations provides an effective way to meet thousands of activists, scholars, and key political figures in every issue area from all over the world. At WCAR there were 10,000 NGO delegates; the forthcoming World Summit on Sustainable Development is expected to draw 30,000 to 50,000. At WCAR I met important activists, organizers, scholars, and progressive representatives of Third World governments from many nations in the world as well as making more than 100 new contacts from the U.S. antiracist movement.

Networking alone is not a strategy, but it is great tactic for those who have a strategy. At the Labor/Community Strategy Center, for example, we now have a key list of more than 200 new international contacts that were derived from the work at WCAR and WSSD PrepComs. Documents and emails are circulating, and some of the WCAR people will also be coming to Johannesburg. There is not now any socialist or communist international body or antiracist international organization. If we have a strategy that focuses on the needs and interests of the Global South against the G8 world dominators, the UN is a critical place to test its possibilities.

The UN allows us to understand the behavior of governments and the many contradictions among them, to watch UN representatives as real people, to observe the palace intrigues among them, and through trial and error, to learn the few instances when NGO pressure, or simply the governments' own contradictions with each other, can move things in a positive direction. For example, in the ICC story, one should not see the U.S. victory in a one-sided way. It was achieved at great costs to its imperial interests. It is not smart politics to humiliate your allies. Every country, rich or poor, big or small, that was forced to change its vote under pressure from the United States dreams of paying the U.S. back. One should not think, for example, that the governments of China or Mexico do not hope to be greater world powers and do not tell themselves that they are only biding their time until more fortuitous conditions arise to challenge U.S. hegemony. We should not see the struggle among the world's governments as simply a puppet show run by the U.S. The U.S. "winner take all" politics—from defying Kyoto to threatening nuclear first-strikes—reflects the overextension of the empire and offers possible points of strategic resistance.

The UN NGO structures offer tactical opportunities to challenge U.S. policies. At Durban, the UN provided an entire structure for NGO organizing, including a massive cricket stadium in which NGOs could assemble, the opportunity to develop their own parallel NGO Forum Declaration and Programme of Action, and some access to the UN governmental structures—if only through considerable struggle. At the May/June 2002 Bali PrepCom for WSSD, the UN organized "multi-stakeholder" dialogues and many structures by which NGOs could put forth their politics and try to impact the governments. The UN is a very promising arena, all things considered, for strengthening international grassroots connections, even if at a later point in history more effective structures and opportunities supercede it.

At the recent UN PrepCom at Bali, an angry NGO delegate complained to Dr. Emil Salim, the Chairman of the Commission on Sustainable Development Bureau in charge of the Preparatory Committees for the WSSD, "Why should we come to the UN when the governments don't listen to us? I just returned from the World Social Forum in Porto Alegre, Brazil, and we were able to lay out a whole vision of a new world we want. We had a chance to speak, we were listened to." Salim rebuked him, "Fine. So if you want to go to a conference of Leftists where you debate strategies that is fine. But when you finish with that strategy, now what do you do? Here is where the power is, here is where the governments are, and you either can or can't get them to listen to you, you either can or can't change their policies. But this is where the challenge is. I can't make them listen to you, that's your job." [22]

---

22. CSD Bureau Chair Emil Salim, statement to NGO delegates at PrepCom IV, Bali International Convention Center, Bali, Indonesia, 26 May 2002.

For the foreseeable future, international conferences, both inside and outside UN aegis, addressing racism, human rights, trade, environment, women's liberation, Indigenous peoples rights, world peace and world war are critical arenas for organizing. Any serious grassroots movement rooted in a major constituency has to develop an explicit international organizing strategy. The UN is one important venue in which to carry it out.

Also, the UN holds conferences at important international locations—key meeting spots for building an antiracist anti-imperialist movement. Remember that it was not just the World Conference Against Racism but the World Conference Against Racism in Durban, South Africa. The forthcoming WSSD will be held in Johannesburg, South Africa. The Strategy Center chose to pay great attention to the World Summit on Sustainable Development because our work has a strong emphasis on challenging environmental racism and fighting for environmental justice but also because we wanted to make a "one-year round trip from Durban to Johannesburg" and deepen our ties to South African political forces and South African society. For many of us at Durban, just walking on the ground of a free South Africa, under Black majority rule was a mind-blowing and life-changing experience—a model of a society in which talking and doing politics is deep in the daily life of the popular culture, something that is hard to imagine in the United States.

At the WSSD PrepCom IV in Bali, Indonesia, a "tourist paradise" distorted by Western as well as Eastern economic domination (U.S., England, Australia, New Zealand, Malaysia, and Taiwan), we met hundreds of activists from the Indonesian People's Forum as well as key organizers from the Philippines, Malaysia, and India. The PrepComs for WSSD held at UN headquarters in New York have not been nearly as valuable for U.S. delegates because very few NGOs from the Third World come to them. The critics of NGO opportunism have trenchantly observed, "Join an NGO and see the world." Still, for U.S. organizers in particular, breaking out of a U.S. frame and seeing the world through the eyes of the oppressed nations gives far greater meaning and intensity to concepts of international solidarity, as well as a much broader perspective on organizing in the U.S. We saw Black women in South Africa standing on the highway, risking their safety to stand in traffic for an entire day to sell, hopefully, five or ten giant avocados for perhaps ten rand ($1). We saw groups of 20 men in Bali pulling massive telephone cables by hand in a coordinated work team, giving the distinct impression of a prison chain gang, in which their pay would be unimaginably low for back-breaking labor. The UN has created important arenas of international participation. It is the job of an aspiring movement to grab those opportunities, and with a sense of orientation and power rooted in a grassroots base on the ground, to learn how to operate in an adversarial international arena with big governments and big business.

One of Durban's greatest achievements was to give greater visibility and moral authority to the anti-imperialist wing of the antiracist movement, and in particular to strengthen actual links between the Black Liberation Movement in the U.S. and the African liberation movements. There has always been a strategic struggle among forces that, broadly construed, could be called "the world antiracist movement." There is a struggle between a pro-imperialist civil rights strategy and an anti-imperialist, antiracist, civil rights and national liberation strategy.

The form of that debate I am most familiar with has been sharply delineated within the Black community in the U.S. The dominant view for most of U.S. history has been the pro-imperialist demand for "equality within the empire," most explicitly advocated by forces within the civil rights establishment. For example, the NAACP, in its pleadings in front of the Supreme Court in *Brown v. Board of Education*, argued that racial equality was in the interests of the U.S. in its fight against the communists. They urged that civil rights could be a tactic with which to win the Cold War.

A decade later, the civil rights establishment, tied as it was to the Democratic Party and the ideology of "loyal Americanism," supported the genocidal war in Vietnam. Many group such as the NAACP and Urban League, up until anti-war sentiment in the Black community became dominant, tried to trade off a hoped-for progress for Blacks "at home" in return for allowing young Black men to fight, kill and die in a war against Third World people. The fledgling Black Left at the time, reflected in Malcolm X and the Student Non-violent Coordinating Committee (SNCC), opposed the war in Vietnam. It said, "Hell No, We Won't Go" to fight in an imperialist war, and articulated the Black Liberation Movement as one for *both* full equality within the U.S. and a revolutionary transformation of U.S. society, including solidarity with the anticolonial movements against the U.S. government. The general transformation from "civil rights" to "Black liberation" was not simply rhetorical. It articulated a new strategic and ideological view that Black people in the U.S. were an oppressed people—for some a Third World people, an African people, an oppressed nation—with rights to self-determination.

Similarly, Malcolm X argued that the U.S. Black Liberation Movement needed to expand its demands for "civil rights"—that is, legal equality inside the U.S.—to "human rights," a framework for demands that could be brought to the UN and other international bodies. Malcolm's argument, rooted in revolutionary Black nationalism, was based on the idea that *Black people in the U.S. had certain inalienable and national rights that the U.S. government could not subjugate nor adjudicate.* This analysis was extended by the demand of the Black Panther Party for a plebiscite of Black people to determine their relationship to the U.S., reflecting that Black people had separate national rights, had a voluntary and conditional relationship to U.S. society that they could terminate if they so chose, and had the right to establish structures for Black people independent of the U.S. government. The tradition from SNCC to Malcolm X to the Black Panthers (rooted in the prior work of W.E.B. DuBois, among many others) reflected the view that *the effective fight for civil rights had to be embedded in the struggle for self-determination and sovereignty for oppressed nations and peoples.*

The leadership of the Black Liberation Movement at that time influenced the revolutionary tendencies within the Chicano, Puerto Rican, Asian/Pacific Islander, and Indigenous peoples movements, whose advocates argued that U.S. racism was tied to *a structural national oppression* which in turn led to a concept of "solidarity" between oppressed peoples inside the U.S. and those in the Third World. The Black Liberation Movement also transformed the lives of tens of thousands of antiracist whites who debated about the best tactics for directly challenging the racist practices of U.S. society in direct alliance with and support for the programmatic

Oppressed ppl in US are like a "Third world ppl"

demands for self-determination of Black, Latino, Asian/Pacific Islander, and Indigenous peoples and communities.

Today, we live at a time of profound counter-revolution, and many ideas that were once ascendant and even dominant in oppressed nationality communities have been suppressed and subjugated, as have the organizations and individuals who once advocated them. From 1980 on, we endured 12 years of the most virulent racist Reagan/Bush Administrations. This was followed by eight years of the Clinton Administration systematically working, often with great success, to cultivate and co-opt a Black and Latino political elite by encouraging it to tie its fortunes to the Democratic Party and world imperialism. This growing Black and Latino comprador bourgeoisie has contributed to enormous suffering for working class and low-income people of color, while many Black and Latino Democratic and now Republican operatives are playing a destructive role as agents of imperialism in Africa and Latin America.

As these relatively small Black and Latino elites enrich themselves at the expense of their own people, there is a break in the multi-class united front for civil rights. The Black and Latino working classes are losing hard fought civil rights on a daily basis—as almost two million people, more than 60 percent of whom are Black and Latino, languish in U.S. prisons. Meanwhile, the Black, Latino, and Asian/Pacific Islander working class, many of whose members are women and immigrants, suffer growing economic exploitation and political repression. They are trying to organize their own movements and organizations of resistance—some "national in form," others multiracial including antiracist whites, to challenge the hegemony of white supremacy, U.S. imperialism, and the treachery of pro-imperialist elites of every nationality. But this is very difficult, for the struggle for national liberation still requires a multi-class united front, and the leadership of the working class of color would be strengthened by more allies from the professional and middle classes of color as well as greater antiracist, pro-working class politics among progressive whites.

The dominant, pro-imperialist line has been in bold relief in U.S. politics after September 11, in which the entire Democratic Party, most of the civil rights establishment, and virtually the entire Congressional Black Caucus—with the notable and heroic exceptions of Barbara Lee and Cynthia McKinney—have lined up with the Bush Administration. They have offered no moral or political leadership against the saturation bombing of the civilian population in Afghanistan or the proto-fascist moves of the Bush Administration at home.

This effort to separate antiracism from anti-imperialism was also operative in Durban. There were forces in the United Nations bureaucracy, in anticipation of strong reactionary pressure from the Western governments, who tried to give WCAR a soft line on racism. They focused on individual stories of "victims' experiences of racism" as a reflection of individual and group irrationality and superiority complexes and thereby decontextualized painful experiences from their structural and colonial roots, the context that would establish the need for the most radical and structural redress and reparations.

The final NGO document, while unable to serve as a powerful on-the-spot tactic for intervention with the governments, was generally representative of the sentiments of the mass of attendees in that it presented a strong anticolonial content. In Durban, the power of the South African Left in its demonstrations against neoliberalism (both COSATU and the Durban Social Forum), the demonstrations of the U.S. delegates against the U.S. walk-out, the active organizing by the Palestinians, and the preeminent moral and political leadership of Fidel Castro and the government of Cuba set a powerful anti-imperialist tone that became the dominant political discourse of the NGO conference. This momentary vision of a world antiracist, anti-imperialist united front, even in its constituent parts as of yet unrealized as a coordinated whole, was very encouraging. It remains to be seen whether those momentary unities can be consolidated organizationally in the years after Durban. But the antiracist, anti-imperialist united front and its challenge to the power and brutality of U.S. and Western imperialism did exist, at a very large scale, on an international stage, at least for a few days. The challenge of course is how to build on those partial understandings, momentary organizational breakthroughs, and new alliances made by groups all over the world. Still, in a world filled with capitalist pollution, ideological and material, the World Conference Against Racism was a breath of fresh air.

I end this sum-up with an excerpt from Fidel Castro's speech to the NGOs at Durban, a model, in microcosm, of the unapologetic voices needed to change the world:

> Nobody has the right to sabotage this conference which, in some way, is attempting to alleviate the terrible suffering and enormous injustice that these deeds have signified and still signify for the overwhelming majority of humanity. Far less does anybody have the right to impose conditions, and demand that the issue of historical responsibility and just reparations are not even mentioned, or the way in which we decide to qualify the horrific genocide at this very minute being committed against our sister

nation of Palestine on the part of extreme-right leaders who, in alliance with the hegemonic superpower, are currently acting in the name of another people which, for close to 2000 years, was the victim of the greatest persecution, discrimination and injustice committed in history.

When Cuba talks of compensation and supports this idea as an ineludible moral duty to the victims of racism, it has an important precedent in the compensation being received by the descendents of those very Jewish peoples who, right in the heart of Europe, suffered an odious and brutal racist holocaust. However, it is not with the intent of attempting the impossible search for direct family members or concrete countries of origin of the victims in terms of deeds that occurred over centuries. The real and irrefutable fact is that tens of millions of Africans were captured, sold like merchandise and dispatched to the other side of the Atlantic to work as slaves, and that 70 million native Indians died in the western hemisphere as a consequence of European conquest and colonization.

The inhuman exploitation to which people of the three continents, including Asia, were subjected, has affected the destiny and present-day life of over 4.5 billion persons inhabiting the Third World nations, and whose indices of poverty, unemployment, infant mortality, life prospects and other disasters impossible to enumerate in a brief speech, are both shocking and horrifying. These are the current victims of that barbarity that lasted for centuries, and the unmistakable creditors of reparations for the horrendous crimes committed against their ancestors and peoples.[23]

I will keep you posted.

---

23. Fidel Castro, key-note address for the closing ceremony of the WCAR NGO Forum, 1 September 2001.

Bulletin from Bali: What Are We Going to Do About the United States?

Author's note: This year, in late August 2002, the United Nations will hold the World Summit on Sustainable Development (WSSD), an international conference in Johannesburg, South Africa, ostensibly to create a new model of sustainable development that integrates economic development, social justice, and environmental imperatives. WSSD is supposed to be a ten year follow-up and implementation conference to the 1992 Rio de Janeiro UN Conference on Environment and Development—thus, its other name, "Rio plus Ten." Just as I attended last year's World Conference Against Racism (WCAR) in Durban, South Africa, I will be going to Johannesburg as part of a delegation from the Labor/Community Strategy Center, as well as commenting as a journalist on these important international developments (we will email and web-post those commentaries throughout the summit). At WCAR last year, and in the Preparatory Committee (PrepCom) meetings that have preceded WSSD, a common theme has emerged—the United States government is bound and determined to undermine, overthrow, and sabotage any international treaties, agreements, and conferences that it believes restrict its sovereignty in any way as the world's rogue superpower. This is the latest chapter of the story, filed from the United Nations PrepCom in Bali, Indonesia, which Strategy Center organizers Cynthia Rojas, Tammy Bang Luu and I attended from late May until early June 2002.

By the second day of the UN's Bali PrepCom, most delegates from the Non-Governmental Organizations (NGOs) oscillated between disgust and depression. The "Chairman's Report"—the summary language that all the world governments were trying to agree upon—was little more than a neoliberal anti-environmental agenda. Naty Bernardino of the International South Group Network called it "Rio minus Ten." As the governmental delegates were debating the language for the final declaration, an angry UN official, thinking his microphone had been turned off, was overheard lamenting, "What are we going to do about the United States?"

Within hours, creative NGO organizers had printed small, paper strips that we pinned to our shirts, repeating that same question. Even that tiny protest was overruled by the UN security force. We were advised by UN staff that any protests inside the Bali International Convention Center (BICC) criticizing a specific government by name would not be permitted—especially one particular government. At the daily NGO meeting the next morning, we were warned by a high ranking UN official that there was a rumor that t-shirts bearing the slogan "What are we going to do about the United States?" would be appearing, and anyone wearing them on the premises would be escorted out. Indeed, one of the organizers was able to have such shirts printed overnight.

Now, many delegates had flown to Bali to advance very specific agendas, representing various groups that had devoted considerable resources to the trip. Although they wanted to wear the t-shirts in protest, they were afraid to risk expulsion. Yet forbidden fruit is always the sweetest. Most NGO delegates, when told they weren't allowed to wear the t-shirts, decided they just had to. The question then was how to advance the tactic—t-shirt civil disobedience. Our dynamic organizing committee, initiated by members of the Women's Caucus, came up with a new tactical wrinkle. We would wear the t-shirts into the Conference Center, but would use masking tape to cover up the "United States" so the t-shirts would read: "What are we going to do about _____?" Aesthetically and politically, the masking of the t-shirts drew greater attention to our message: the U.S. was running the show, and our protest of its hegemony was being censored. The life and death fight against the policies of the United States had taken center stage at Bali.

Many groups had come to the Bali PrepCom to demand "water as a human right." The U.S. refused; it argued that water is a commodity to be privatized.

Groups had demanded that the U.S. sign the Kyoto treaty and that WSSD pass a proposal for a far more radical reduction in greenhouse gases than the five percent proposed by Kyoto. The U.S. refused to sign Kyoto altogether, and opposed any language linking fossil fuel combustion to global warming thereby blocking any efforts to save the small island states and the entire planet from ecological catastrophe.

NGOs and even a few governments had demanded binding language with specific timetables and goals, such as reducing world poverty by 50 percent by the year 2015. The U.S. opposed specific numerical goals, specific timetables, structures of accountability, or penalties for noncompliance.

NGOs—trying to impact the document by influencing governments—asked for strong and binding international language to restrict transnational corporations' production of carcinogens, mining in indigenous communities, and production of oil. The U.S. argued that any corporate behavior must be "voluntary," that the principle of national sovereignty not international law should shape the Johannesburg meeting. Any agreements between governments and corporations, argued the U.S., should be based on nonbinding public/private "partnerships"—the ideological poison pill. But even on the issue of "protecting national sovereignty," the U.S. was hypocritical. The U.S. *did* propose international and binding rules by the World Trade Organization (WTO) against indigenous and Third World nations trying to protect their own industries and sovereignty from the penetration of oil, mining, and agricultural transnationals. The U.S. supported protective tariffs for its own steel industry and supported massive subsidies to its agricultural multinationals in order to tear down the domestic industries of other nations. For the U.S. government and its present embodiment in the Bush administration, no principles exist: international rules to regulate transnational corporations, no but international rules to advance neoliberalism, yes. It is simply a question of which formulation best advances its imperial interests.

Worse, the U.S. would tolerate no dissent. It was known to be bullying every government in private "green room" shakedowns—even demanding the Norwegian ambassador to the U.S. censor the courageous Norwegian UN ministers at Bali who were fighting for international treaties to control transnational corporate abuses and to support indigenous peoples' rights. And every time governments put forth progressive language, the U.S. put the statements in "brackets," which is the UN procedure for contesting and trying to remove policies with which a government doesn't agree. For these and many other reasons, the question remained: "What are we going to do about the United States?"

On Wednesday afternoon, May 29th, more than 50 delegates went to the Greenpeace ship docked at Bali harbor. In front of some local media, we finally ripped off the masking tape from the previously censored t-shirts, exposing the "United States." Several of our spokespeople, including Canadian organizer Prabha Khosla from the Women's Caucus and Henry Shillingford from the Caribbean, talked about how the U.S. was sabotaging any positive outcomes for environmental justice at WSSD.

The U.S.—threatening each nation with economic, political and, if necessary, military retaliation—is imposing an anti-regulatory agenda on the conference. The governmental groups, from the European Union to the G77 & China (the nations of the Global South), are unable or unwilling to offer an organized opposition. The U.S. is working to undermine the Johannesburg summit by substituting worthless voluntary agreements for enforceable ones, continuing to impose business and trade dictatorships (pushed through by the U.S. at the Doha and Monterey world trade conferences over dependent nations) and formalizing the stealing of indigenous land, property rights, and cultures. Ask any person working at WSSD on any subject—human rights, water, biodiversity, energy, global warming or debt cancellation—and they will tell you the same thing: the U.S is "bracketing" our lives, ruling all progress out of order.

How ironic that in the midst of all this heavy-handed repression, the main objective of the U.S. and UN is to come out of Johannesburg with an emphasis on "partnerships." According to this argument, Rio in 1992 failed because it was too restrictive of corporate rights. Now, the U.S wants the delegates to denounce specific regulations to stop mining or oil exploration and instead propose "partnerships"—the grand illusion of our time— between NGOs and corporations like Shell Oil.

Our tiny t-shirt protest was well below the scope and scale needed to impact policy or any balance of power, but as a microcosm of what is urgently needed in Johannesburg and back in the U.S., it was an important beginning. Building on the important anti-globalization protests against transnational corporations, it focused on the U.S. government and its many

henchmen—Japan, Canada, Australia, and New Zealand...
Ooops, there I go again mentioning governments by name. It
broke with the sterile wordsmithing of UN conferences that would
drive most grassroots organizers into years of psychotherapy.
And, because effective leadership groups are essential, it was
great to be part of a multiracial, international working group with
such strong women's leadership.

The dilemmas facing us and the world are almost too painful to confront. Many progressives are well aware of the
reactionary role of international agencies dominated by the
U.S.—the G8, WTO, IMF, and World Bank. But don't forget
the U.S. Army, NATO and CIA are also helping to turn the
world into the dreaded "company store" of the Pullman rail-
road empire in which the workers grew "another day older and
deeper in debt." Under these global conditions, some
grassroots organizers and NGOs are so disgusted at the results
of Bali they are asking themselves what the value is of walking
into a card game in Johannesburg where the U.S. is the dealer
and the deck is stacked.

For those of us who *do* plan to take a stand at Johannesburg,
all of our work should be framed by one overriding objective—
building an international movement that focuses on
self-determination for the oppressed and dependent nations of
the global South and that challenges the domination and abuses
of the U.S. In Johannesburg, if you focus exclusively on trying
to amend the specific language of the final UN governmental
document you will be bitterly disappointed, because the U.S. will
get what it wants—that is a predetermined outcome. But a significant anti-imperialist victory is possible. We need a major and

public confrontation with the United States government and its free market madness in Johannesburg, and after that, we must organize long-term campaigns against corporate and superpower abuse. It is essential that the international press and our constituencies at home come to understand that WSSD is imposing a death sentence on billions of people through continued and even greater levels of pollutants and poverty. As we prepare for Johannesburg, you should ask yourself "What are *you* going to do about the United States?"

I will keep you posted.

Bringing It All Back Home: The Strategy Center a Year After Durban

The World Conference Against Racism and the South African movements raised profound challenges for all of us who attended WCAR. After romantic dreams of staying in South Africa, I remember having a conversation with Cindy Weisner of People Organized to Win Employment Rights (POWER), based in San Francisco, about what we would do differently once we returned to the U.S. How could this go beyond a dream series in a movie, beyond a "feeling" of transformation to actual changes in our work and our lives? How could we repay our South African and Third World hosts? What were our international obligations?

Just before I left for WCAR, the Strategy Center's Program Demand Group published a new edition of *Toward a Program of Resistance*, built on 24 key anti-imperialist demands that asked the U.S. Left to challenge our own government. I distributed the document in Durban to indicate that there were folks in the United States, in L.A., who were looking for ways to stand up to the empire, looking for international issues, causes, and alliances. In this dispatch, I will describe the work of my own organizations, the Labor/Community Strategy Center and the Bus Riders Union, and explain concrete changes reflected in new projects and new ways of thinking about our work, that are direct results of the transformative impact of the Durban experience and the challenges of the post-September 11 reaction.

Building a Grassroots Base

It is hard to imagine building a movement against an imperialist empire when widespread disillusionment with the political process exists. Black people have long been alienated and excluded from the formal electoral political process. Mexican, Central American, and Asian refugees and immigrants understand that the system has use for their low-wage labor, but not their ideas or their interests. Although building a movement among the urban poor and the low-wage working class is difficult, that is where our work in the Bus Riders Union/Sindicato de Pasajeros (BRU/SDP) is rooted. These are the people who are our members and our leaders, all of whom are at the core of our political experiment. For some of the riders we approach on the bus with our grand dreams and schemes—oppressed people who are working every waking moment just to survive—the idea of any form of political action, let alone challenging the Bush juggernaut, let alone "building the Left," seems like a concept from another planet. Still, when we try to imagine an antiracist resistance, it must start with some real people whose daily lives create the material conditions that could possibly compel them or propel them into radical political activism.

At the Strategy Center, our work focuses on building mass movements of the working class, with a particular emphasis on developing leadership from the low-income working class in Los Angeles which is overwhelmingly Black, Latino, and Asian/Pacific Islander, women, and immigrants. Only from such a grassroots base can we even imagine demanding that the United States stop its interventions.

From 1982-1992, the predecessor to the Strategy Center, the Labor/Community Coalition to Keep GM Van Nuys Open, organized a powerful antiracist movement rooted in a 5,000 person, predominantly Latino and Black United Auto Workers (UAW) auto plant in Los Angeles. We tried to carry out in practice the strategic alliance of the multinational working class and the oppressed nationality communities, in this case an alliance of the GM Van Nuys workers and L.A.'s Chicano and Black communities. We utilized the tactic of a pre-emptive boycott of GM cars in greater Los Angeles which was the largest new car market in the United States at that time. We raised the antiracist civil rights demand that GM had an obligation to keep decent-paying union jobs in L.A for Chicano, Black, and women workers, all of whom were always the last hired and the first fired. To even our own amazement, we forced GM to keep the plant open an entire decade longer than it had planned.[1]

From 1989-1993, the Strategy Center initiated an environmental justice group, the WATCHDOG, that initiated a "Clean Up the Refineries, Fight Environmental Racism" campaign in the Harbor area of Los Angeles. Predominantly low-income, Latino immigrant residents were subjected to lethal emissions from a battery of oil refineries in the area—Shell, Unocal, Ultramar, Chevron, and Texaco. Two years after our organizing began, the Texaco refinery exploded, luckily killing no one, but raging in flames for an entire day and exposing nearby residents to shock, smoke, and chemical inhalation. The WATCHDOG built a strong L.A. County community-based movement. It challenged the regional environmental agency, the South Coast Air Quality Management District (AQMD), by demanding a 50 percent reduction in Texaco emissions, a neighborhood health clinic for environmental diseases as well as reparations to Ecuador for Texaco's "drill and run" abuses, a demand rooted in an alliance we formed with Acción Ecológica in Ecuador.[2] At its height, the WATCHDOG had several hundred active members and a core of 25 community residents helping to lead the organization and the movement. Out of that work, we participated actively in the

---

1. Eric Mann, *Taking on General Motors: A Case Study of the UAW Campaign to Keep GM Van Nuys Open* (Los Angeles: UCLA Institute of Industrial Relations, 1987).

2. Kikanza Ramsey, Geoff Ray, and Rita Burgos, along with filmmakers Mark Dworkin and Melissa Young, went on a Strategy Center delegation to Ecuador, where they strategized with Acción Ecológica organizers. The WATCHDOG Environmental Justice campaign is captured in the film, *Voices from the Frontlines* (available at Strategy Center publications, www.thestrategycenter.org).

National People of Color Environmental Justice Leadership Summit in 1991. Our organizing strategy began with building a strong working class base in a megacity of ten million people. From there we reached out to environmental justice groups rooted in communities of color in the United States and to social movements in oppressed nations in the Third World to challenge U.S.-based transnational corporations and the governmental structures that protected their interests.

From 1993 to the present, the Strategy Center's main work has focused on building the L.A. Bus Riders Union/Sindicato de Pasajeros. The story of how we built this movement will fill a future book. It includes a ground-breaking civil rights case—the *Labor/Community Strategy Center and Bus Riders Union, et al. v. Los Angeles MTA* in which we charged the MTA with violating Title VI of the 1964 Civil Rights Act.[3] The suit resulted in a civil rights Consent Decree, signed by the MTA, that not only won reduced fares and the promise of more buses, but also legally established the BRU as the "class representative" for 400,000 daily bus riders. In that settlement, the courts and even the MTA acknowledged that since the MTA had violated bus riders' civil rights, the BRU had the right and obligation to represent them.

Over eight years, the BRU has evolved a complex urban organizing strategy—using many tactics in the ebb and flow of the campaign—to build the ideological and organizational capacity

---

3. *Labor/Community Strategy Center, et al., v. Los Angeles County Metropolitan Transportation Authority*, CV 94-5936 TJH (MCx), available from www.thestrategycenter.org. For a lengthier discussion see "Conclusion: The Left Choice is the Best Choice."

and leadership of a multiracial working class organization. Our tactical arsenal includes a "No Seat No Fare, Don't Pay for Racism" campaign in which the BRU organized a "fare strike" to protest overcrowding on the bus and the MTA's refusal to abide by the Consent Decree, a 100-person traffic-blocking sit-in to protest the MTA's cuts in night service, and a student/youth campaign to force the MTA to make student bus passes widely accessible. In each campaign, we have won or are winning our demands. Focusing on what we call "consciousness, leadership, and organization," we use the slogan, "we'd rather have 2,000 new members than 2,000 new buses." Ironically, or, better yet, ideologically, that formulation has allowed us to accomplish both.

The BRU is a relatively small organization by 1960s standards, but a fairly large one in the midst of 21st century political reaction. The BRU begins with a 12-person leadership body, the Planning Committee, and another center of tactical leadership, the Action Committee, with its core of 15 people. The BRU general membership meets monthly, with attendance that ranges from 50 to 100, and new members in that meeting, as many as 30, have their own orientation. The BRU retains an active core of 200 people, 100 of whom are very active, and has recruited more than 3,000 dues-paying members. In over eight years of work we have cultivated a core constituency of 50,000 on-the-bus supporters. It is from that base, and the theory of placing membership recruitment, training, and education at the center of our work, that we have won more than 2,200 clean fuel buses from the MTA, replacing 2,200 dilapidated diesel buses—a major victory for environmental justice. But the constant challenge to us, on the front lines of our work, is the building of a multiracial working class organization.

On many days, the Bus Riders Union sends five full-time organizers, five organizers-in-training, and as many as 15 active members out on the buses of Los Angeles. They talk to, or at least try to talk to, hundreds of bus riders who are on their way to work, school, recreation, hospitals, or home from jail. Many bus riders are monolingual Spanish or Korean speakers, and they are immigrants from Korea, El Salvador, Nicaragua, Guatemala, the Philippines, or Mexico—many, many from Mexico. They are community college and high school students, domestic, garment, hotel, and restaurant workers, welfare recipients, the elderly and the disabled.

In eight years of organizing, our work, like that of most grassroots groups, has focused on what could be seen as group interested demands—that is, lower bus fares, an end to diesel buses, dramatic reductions in overcrowding, and the building of a bus riders movement. The material gains for the urban working class, a reflection of the powerful combination of a class action lawsuit and organizing grassroots pressure, have been substantial. Over eight years of organizing, we have gone well beyond fighting "cutbacks" to turning the bus system on its head. Imagine 2,200 brand new compressed natural gas buses at a cost of almost one billion dollars, significant reductions in overcrowding, a new $11 weekly bus pass, and a $42 monthly pass. The MTA has not raised bus fares for six years out of fear of our movement.

Transformative organizing is rooted in the fight for the people's livelihoods, democratic rights, and daily survival. It is where working class people develop the first stages of class consciousness in the direct struggle with the corporate class and the capitalist state. It is where working class people deepen their analysis of the system from self-interested grievances to a structural analysis of their enemies and their own location in a class, race and gender stratified society. It is where the working class people move from a general critique of "the system" or even "imperialism" to the difficult tactical questions of a war of position, a war of maneuver, a long-term class struggle, and a class war. It is where working people learn about united fronts and tactical alliances, and develop their own skills and creativity in the endless daily skirmishes and longer campaigns, winning real victories, partial as they may be, to understand that the system can be beat, if only temporarily until the next conflict. It is where working class people test their own "class stand" and begin to look inward at their own racial and gender dynamics, their own internal struggles and demons, and their own rivers to cross. It is the base from which a solid internationalism can be built, the foundation of their own oppression, direct experience, and class consciousness. Ultimately, we have always measured our success by how hard this group of Bus Riders Union members fights for a broader class interest that is not, or may not be, in their immediate group or individual interests.

That is why we are challenging ourselves to practice a more explicit and consistent internationalism; this is one of the key lessons of WCAR for our work. This lesson was imprinted on my brain in the streets of South Africa: we have to remind ourselves time and time again that "class consciousness" means putting forth a transformative internationalist politics based on a broader class interest. It is *the entire world working class*, not just the working class and oppressed peoples in the U.S., that requires a worldwide united front fight against empire and against U.S. imperialism, as the key strategic objective.

The Ideological and Professional Training of Organizers

The Strategy Center is the home of the National School for Strategic Organizing, which admits five to six organizers per class for a six-month intensive practice and theory immersion into the world of grassroots organizing. We define an organizer as "the smallest single unit around whom you can build a larger form of organization."[4] We help the organizers aspire to that role and learn to carry it out. The vast majority of organizers we recruit are Black, Latino, and Asian/Pacific Islander as well as antiracist whites, usually majority women, some already Bus Riders Union members, and all with previous histories of activism.

At the height of the civil rights and anti-war movements of the 1960s, millions of young people and people of all ages joined the movement, but at the heart of every movement were actual organizations, and at the heart of the organizations were the organizers—going block-to-block in the urban core, door-to-door among rural sharecroppers, and room-to-room in the college dorms, having one-on-one conversations with real people, recruiting a grassroots base, and building a new cadre of leaders one conversation and one person at a time. And yet it was the mass events of history—the Freedom Rides, the Selma March, the March on Washington, the Columbia strike against the war, the student battle of the Pentagon, and the Mississippi Freedom Democratic Party challenge, that recruited thousands of people at a time—the epoch-shaping events that most people would point to as the day they became "radicalized."

---

4. Eric Mann, "The Role of the Conscious Organizer," National School for Strategic Organizing Training Document, 2001.

Increasingly, as many of the applicants to our school come to us with impressive organizing experience, we have come to see the National School as a "graduate school" for already gifted young organizers, what Goh Chien Yen from Singapore and the Third World Network called "an academy" when he first heard about it. We need people who can write and orate, go on a bus and talk to dozens of people in English, Spanish, and Korean, then come back to the office to call new contacts, write and design a leaflet, and work with members to build new leadership structures, carry out existing projects, and help initiate new ones. (All applicants must be bilingual and many of our Black organizers in particular have studied Spanish as a part of their work at the Strategy Center to become viable and sometimes fluent bilingual organizers.)

The School curriculum pivots on the "organizers' exchange" and the "political strategy and tactics seminar" so that students are trained to think long-term and evolve their own macro analysis, as well as learn to apply that theory to their daily practice. We are very supportive of other organizations, like the Center for Third World Organizing (CTWO), who have developed their own theories and institutions for organizer training. We need such training programs because there are now hundreds of dedicated and gifted young people throughout the U.S., many of whom are women and people of color, who are already working on sweatshop labor issues, anti-globalization, antiracist, and environmental justice community-based campaigns, and who want to take their work to another level.

The legacy of Durban involves big picture organizing and the training of long distance runners. I once heard that at a moment when the South African anti-Apartheid struggle was facing massive government repression, it was said that you should not join the struggle if you would not invest decades, because you could not overthrow the Apartheid regime in years. It could take generations. The movement had to make the long-term commitment that Apartheid must go, no matter how long it would take. In that spirit, over the last ten years of our work we have worked to train 55 organizers.

The United Nations as an Arena of Work

One of the lessons of WCAR was that you cannot just show up at a UN international conference and expect to play an effective organizational role. The UN, like all institutions, has an organizational culture, ground rules, procedures, and mechanisms that one has to master in order to be effective. The Strategy Center made the decision, after working at WCAR, that if we wanted to work in a UN conference, we would have to make an organizational investment to attend the many PrepComs that are usually a year or more of international meetings, which precede these high visibility UN showcases. Every UN conference ultimately ends with a decision by the governments, and there are endless drafts of documents that are edited and re-edited over the year. Sometimes there is an NGO document to parallel the government document (as there was at WCAR); sometimes there is only an official government document that the NGOs have to try to impact through lobbying and pressuring governments to adopt their proposals.

At an earlier stage in our organization's development, investing this much time into UN work would not have been a good move; there was a base to build, an organization to create. But, we've found that as we approach international work from an already constructed regional base, the UN is a productive and valuable arena of work—not the centerpiece, but valuable nonetheless.

This time, in preparation for the World Summit on Sustainable Development (WSSD), the Strategy Center has attended three PrepComs—two at the UN in New York and one in Bali, Indonesia. Even as we try to assess whether we can have any impact on the governmental document or process, so far completely dominated by the U.S. and the EU, we have met with several hundred NGO leaders from all over the world. Even a few weeks at the UN can be a mind-blowing consciousness raising experience. People in Asia, Africa, and Latin America start describing in vivid and historical detail their accounts of the AIDS epidemic, the immediate impacts of global warming, the efforts by transnational corporations to privatize their water and their sewage systems, the failure of governments to provide even emergency food, and the corruption and brutality of military dictatorships supported by the United States. They also describe impressive, often heroic grassroots movements of resistance. It has the feel of a language immersion course; you are actually learning a lot but you feel overwhelmed, in this case by the deluge of life and death information.

As we prepare for WSSD in Johannesburg, several of us from the Strategy Center, Cynthia Rojas, Tammy Bang Luu, and I, have been able to play active, and at times, leadership roles in the earlier NGO PrepComs. We have been building greater political agreement and cooperation among NGOs to try to construct an NGO movement—a very hard job. We have been working with the Third World Network and other groups to organize NGO opposition to U.S. proposals for voluntary and co-optive "partnerships" between transnational corporations, governments, and NGOs. We have confronted U.S. governmental delegates in large open sessions of the "multi-stakeholder dialogues" for their sabotage of binding international treaties for pollution and poverty reduction. In Bali, we participated in a creative anti-U.S. demonstration inside and outside the UN (described in Dispatch Number 6, "Bulletin from Bali") and helped coordinate a press conference of 13 different NGO caucuses who agreed upon a common statement challenging corporate control of the UN and the World Summit on Sustainable Development. We are active in the Environmental Justice, Youth, Corporate Accountability, Human Rights, Women's, Corporate Accountability, and Energy caucuses as well as the overall NGO caucus.

Since then, returning home to Smog City, we played an active role in a Los Angeles Town Hall meeting on the World Summit which attracted more than 300 people. Because of our work at the three WSSD PrepComs, I was asked to be one of the plenary speakers and was able to engage in a serious issue-based challenge to the Bush Administration policies with its designated speaker for the event, Alan D. Hecht, director of International Environmental Affairs and member of the National Security Council. I focused on the hypocrisy of the U.S. position at WSSD. On the one hand, the U.S. imposes economic and monetary policies on Third World Nations to their grave detriment, policies the U.S. demands must be binding. On the other hand, the U.S. demands exemption from Kyoto, and from any binding outcomes at WSSD. The U.S. walked out of the World

Us

Conference Against Racism, refused to sign, or abide by, the provisions of the International Criminal Court that prohibit war crimes, and told WSSD that corporations should only enter into "voluntary agreements" to reduce pollutants and toxins, with no timetables, no goals, no enforcement, and no penalties for noncompliance.

Most of the people from L.A. who attended the meeting were traditional, middle class environmentalists from the white West side of town, not at all our core constituency. But they are an important piece of the puzzle nonetheless. They are essential in a broad united front to challenge the Bush Administration and needed to provide greater political cover for the low-income working class of color. Many of these forces, through more than ten years of our outreach to them, have come to support our more militant approach to challenging corporations and our forthright confrontations with the Bush Administration (while having been more uncomfortable with our confrontations with the Clinton/Gore Administration). Others are at least tolerant of our constant emphasis on racism and imperialism and, in their own way, agree with many of the specific programmatic reflections of that analysis—unity in action as we call it. Some of them will also be attending WSSD, and that offers another opportunity to build a broad united front of forces in L.A. that can provide a larger base of support for our future campaigns on global warming and, a least, a receptive audience to our campaigns in support of Palestinian rights and for reparations.

In enthusiastic response to the lessons of WCAR and the progress at WSSD, the Strategy Center and Bus Riders Union decided to send a six person delegation to the World Summit in Johannesburg—BRU Planning Committee Co-Chair Barbara

Lott-Holland, longtime L.A. civil rights activist Woodrow Coleman, Tammy Bang Luu and Cynthia Rojas from the Strategy Center's organizing staff, Lian Hurst Mann from AhoraNow publications, and me. Many of the members of the Bus Riders Union find our new-found work and the issues we bring back from the United Nations fascinating. It is a Cliff Notes for a short course on the world situation, and they are deeply enthusiastic about initiating our new Reparations and Global Warming projects as well as the burgeoning work on the issue of Palestine. The UN work fits in with the internationalist and transformative strategy that drives our grassroots organizing work.

Building a Strategy Center Reparations Project

Even before Durban, the Strategy Center's Program Demand Group had begun focusing more attention on the demand for reparations, but there is no question that WCAR pushed our consciousness to another level. Many of our Black members in particular were so deeply moved by the events at WCAR that they proposed we begin a Strategy Center reparations project. We are beginning a serious study of reparations, reading all the major books and articles on the subject, and investigating the work of groups that have been working on reparations for many years, to learn from their experiences. We have enormous respect for the many historical figures who have, in this recent period, pushed the Reparations Movement to great historical prominence, among them Randall Robinson, founder of TransAfrica and author of *The Debt: What America Owes to Blacks*, Charles Ogletree, Adjoa Aiyetro and many other

prominent legal and academic figures. Out of that study and reflection we will think about what unique role our organization can
play in strengthening the broad united front for reparations as
well as how we can take that work into AhoraNow publications,
the Program Demand Group, the National School for Strategic
Organizing, and the Bus Riders Union. The BRU has a core constituency of 50,000 bus riders from every racial and ethnic group
in the city. This gives the reparations work a pre-existing and
sympathetic social base. In particular, our South L.A. organizing team will be focusing on expanding the Black membership
participation, in that more than 20 percent of L.A.'s 400,000
daily bus riders, 80,000 people, are Black. We want to help
build the Reparations Movement and help bring its revolutionary message to the urban working class.

Building Bus Riders' Support for the Palestinian Struggle

For more than a year before WCAR, two Strategy Center members Layla Welborn and Mizue Aizeki traveled to Palestine and
worked as a two-person political education team on the subject. They conducted excellent, internal popular education based
on moving photos and firsthand narratives. It took the continued escalation of Israeli assaults and the imperatives for action
that came out of WCAR to push our organization to begin a
systematic public education campaign about Palestine in the
Bus Riders Union.

Beginning in April of 2002, the Bus Riders Union Planning
Committee spent a month debating in great detail a position of
the strongest condemnation of Israeli atrocities and support for

the Palestinian Movement. Then we took the draft text of a two-page leaflet to our general membership for a full debate—in English, Spanish, and Korean. After an hour and half of debate, the motion passed 40 to one with eight abstentions. So, we extended the vote for another month, until we had signed up more than 100 key members who were knowledgeable and enthusiastic. Then, as we began to distribute more than 10,000 leaflets on the buses, we still held an internal teach-in for 50 of our most active members that took another Saturday. We do not push Left issues through our membership on a "sounds good" basis. If we were going to take a stand on Palestine we wanted to truly consult with and consolidate our members on both the politics and organizational consequences of our actions. The final public leaflet places most of our demands on our own government, the United States, because we believe that without the more than $5 billion a year in military and economic aid and the clear promise of U.S. military backup, Israel would not be so brazen in its military aggression. The Bus Riders Union demanded:

☐ that the U.S. government end all military and economic aid to Israel; *an end to US funding in Israel*

☐ that the U.S. government stop its sabotage of, and immediately implement UN resolutions 242 and 338, which demand an end to the illegal Israeli occupation of Palestinian land;

☐ that the U.S. government stop its sabotage of, and immediately implement UN resolution 194 which grants the right of return for Palestinian refugees to their homes of origin.

The leaflets are being distributed to thousands of bus riders, in English, Spanish, and Korean, by dozens of organizers, organizers-in-training, and members. After a month of this campaign, the results are mixed, but overall quite positive. Many bus riders have never gotten any information about the Palestinian struggle and are just grateful for being exposed to the issue. Others have strong feelings in support of the Palestinians and are very impressed that the BRU would take on international issues so clearly, and for some, they have greater interest in Palestine than buses. Some bus riders who do not agree with the position are angry with the Palestinians and "the Arabs," and blame them for terrorism. But the goal is not just to gain unanimous acceptance of a "position"; the goal is to bring class consciousness to the working class people on the bus, and to slowly change the class and race nature of support for the Palestinian people, clearly a long-term project for a long-term struggle.

In Los Angeles, there are also demonstrations in front of the Israeli consulate by a small group, L.A. Jews for a Just Peace, that also calls for an end to the U.S. military aid to Israel, an end to the occupation, and the right of return for Palestinians. This challenges the myth of monolithic Jewish support for Israeli atrocities. We understand that a few thousand multilingual leaflets on the bus and relatively small demonstrations by dissident Jews mean little to the Bush Administration and would have meant even less to the Gore/Lieberman Administration. U.S. Middle East policy is motivated by an urgent drive to control the region's oil reserves and even larger geopolitical drives to control the world. In that context, Israel is a key ally of the U.S. imperial interests in the region. So it is no surprise that the Bush Administration continues to manipulate and use "suicide bombing," which is a tactic of survival for Palestinians's desperate struggle for freedom, as a pretext for continued support of Israeli escalation of violence.

In the past five decades, Palestinian national consciousness and a movement for national liberation has grown in response to the Israeli occupation. It is essential to signal to a world community and to the Palestinians in particular that they have allies in the U.S., that Israeli policies are not supported by all Jews, and that there is resistance to U.S. Middle East policies. As with Vietnam, the future of Palestine rests in its own people's hands. As with Vietnam, there is no way they can win the fight alone. In that context, efforts by publications like *War Times*, the large anti-Israeli protests in Europe (the coverage of which the capitalist press is intentionally suppressing), and the nascent efforts of Jews for a Just Peace and the Bus Riders Union are the building blocks of a protracted struggle that must begin by letting the Palestinians know that they are not fighting alone.

Building a Strategy Center Project on Global Warming

One of the conclusions we reached after WCAR was to continue our international work at the World Summit on Sustainable Development. It seems each commitment generates another. When we attended the first PrepCom of WSSD, Cynthia Rojas, an organizer with the Strategy Center, and I attended an educational event organized by representatives of the Organization of Small Island States (OSIS), such as Samoa and Tuvalu. They showed us a deeply moving film, *Rising Waters: Global Warming and the Fate of the Pacific*

Islands, and presented the ecological horror stories about how global warming, primarily from greenhouse gas production from the Western countries, is wreaking havoc on their societies: melting the coral reefs that have protected their shores for thousands of years; driving away the tuna that are the main source of food and local industry; causing floods of such proportions they are wiping out island infrastructure; and depleting their governmental budget to build ocean walls that still do not succeed in keeping the floods at bay.[5]

OSIS asked people in the U.S. to understand that Kyoto's mere five percent reduction in greenhouse gases (which the U.S. government has refused to implement) solves little. A 50 percent reduction in greenhouse gas production today, which is what they are demanding, would still take decades to begin to stabilize and then possibly reverse, some of the worst manifestations of global warming. This demand comes at a time when every U.S. auto manufacturer is shooting for a ten percent *increase* in auto sales year after year and, worse, expanding the production of SUVs and pickup trucks, their biggest money-makers. We have learned that epidemics throughout the Third World, like mosquito-transmitted malaria and dengue fever, as well as droughts and desertification, are being caused or exacerbated by the warming of the earth's atmosphere.[6]

---

5. Andrea Torrice, *Rising Waters: Global Warming and the Fate of Pacific Islands*, 57 mins (Oley, PA: Bulldog Films, 200s0), videocassette: VHS.

6. Paul Epstein "Is Global Warming Harmful to Health?" *Scientific American* (August 2000): 50. Computer models indicate that many diseases will surge as the earth's atmosphere heats up. Signs of the predicted troubles have begun to appear. Epstein is Associate Director, Center for Health and the Global Environment, Harvard Medical School.

This led to our decision, one that we were already contemplating, to initiate a Climate Justice/Global Warming project in Los Angeles, again focusing on the urban core bus riders. This campaign, still in its planning stages, will begin with a public health education campaign, targeting a core constituency of 50,000 bus riders, overwhelmingly Black, Latino, and Korean, highlighting the causal link between auto emissions and childhood asthma, cancer, leukemia, and chronic lung dysfunction among Angelenos. From there, we will try to explain how those same L.A. auto emissions also generate greenhouse gases that in turn lead to the suffering and deaths of people in the Third World. This experiment will, of necessity, bring Bus Riders Union members into a direct collision course with the oil and auto industries and will require international cooperation with public health and environmental justice groups around the world.

Returning to South Africa

When I left the World Conference Against Racism in Durban, South Africa in September 2001, I knew that the gift of that experience had to be shared with other key staff and members. I also knew that there was a strategic reason to return, because Johannesburg would be the site of the UN World Summit on Sustainable Development. This would allow us to expand the international component of our Environmental Justice work and complete a "one-year round trip" from Durban to Johannesburg. In the week before the official governmental summit, we will be participating in a Corporate Accountability Week organized by GroundWork, a South African environmental justice group, among others. We will participate in the International Steering Group which has responsibilities for the NGO Global Peoples

Forum, working with the Third World Network and other NGOs with whom we have been cooperating for a year.

A big part of the attraction is to reconnect with our friends from COSATU, the ANC, and the SACP, as well as those from Khanya College and the Durban Social Forum, even as we are well aware that many of those forces are locked in sharp strategic struggles with each other. We welcome another chance to understand the complex dynamics among all the forces in South Africa, to hear their reactions to September 11, and to watch the internal and external debates continue on the future of the country. Our contribution is to continue to ask the question, "What can we do to help? What actions against the U.S. government can help expand the options for South African self-determination?" For Barbara Lott-Holland and Woodrow Coleman in particular, it is a chance for them to return to their ancestral roots—to stand on African soil, to breathe the air of South African politics. Woodrow, after more than 40 years of activism in L.A.'s Black community, keeps telling us, "I'm going home."

I will keep you posted.

Conclusion:

The Left Choice
Is the Best Choice

SECTION ONE
THE HISTORICAL FRAME:
SEPTEMBER 11TH CHALLENGES THE WORLDWIDE
ANTIRACIST MOVEMENT

Within minutes after the events of September 11, the few remaining left liberals and Leftists in the U.S. understood that the world was in grave danger, as a right-wing government, which had come to power in an electoral coup, moved with impressive reactionary dispatch. The airplane attacks on the World Trade Center would be used by the far-Right as a pretense, a pretext to consolidate a pre-existing agenda: "September 11th" would function just as "Remember the Maine" had been used in the Spanish American war of conquest and the "Gulf of Tonkin" incident had been used to justify further U.S. aggression in Vietnam.

In most incidents of U.S. colonial aggression, a trumped-up story was a sufficient pretense for colonial avarice. "Protecting U.S. citizens" was a bad enough story, but sometimes it was even "protecting U.S. troops." A jingoistic public never met a war it didn't like, and many benefit so much from imperialism that they never chose to ask, "What were our troops doing there in the first place?" This response has a long history that begins with the white settlers murdering their Indigenous hosts—and then celebrating "Thanksgiving." During the genocide in Vietnam, as the U.S. was murdering three million civilians, many "Americans" were furious that the Vietnamese "communists" were killing U.S. troops in self-defense.

Even with this history of popular support for aggression and genocide, the Bush Administration came to power understanding that there were some constraints on its goals of worldwide economic, political, and military conquest. What more fortuitous development could it have imagined than an apparently "unprovoked" attack by "terrorists?" Many Leftists understood that the U.S. had been training right-wing terror groups, often religious, anticommunist fanatics, to undermine and overthrow progressive and left governments throughout the world—including in Afghanistan.[1] We argued that the people in the World Trade Center and the Pentagon had been killed by the U.S. euphemism "friendly fire." That is, they were killed by U.S.-trained troops, as Al Qaeda had been a product of the U.S. CIA. But as Bush moved

---

1. Vijay Prashad, *War Against the Planet: The Fifth Afghan War, Imperialism, and Other Assorted Fundamentals*, (New Delhi: LeftWord Books, 2002). Prashad goes into an excellent analysis of the U.S. campaign, successful in most instances, of wiping out the secular, socialist and communist Left in the Middle East, and replacing it with right-wing, anticommunist, religious fanatics, the source of its present problem.

with aggressiveness and lethal intent, many on the Left, including some who had just returned from Durban, were frightened and disoriented. It had already been so difficult to imagine how to translate the momentary sense of power of an antiracist movement in Durban back to the arch-racist United States, and now this!

Within a day, the Bush Administration moved to use the events to usher in a war against the world, a "war against the planet" as Vandana Shiva calls it.[2] Orlando Rodriguez, a courageous parent whose son Gregory was killed in the World Trade Center, bucking the system's turn to war, called a press conference to declare, "Not with my son's life, you don't."[3] Obviously, had it chosen, the Bush Administration could have called for moderation and restraint in response to the events of September 11, as it has in the prosecution of corporate criminals and white racists. But for the Right, this was no time for restraint, it was the chance of a lifetime.

At the time of the Oklahoma City bombing, I think virtually every Black person, every antiracist in the U.S. prayed, "Please do not be a Black militant, the national witch hunt would be unbearable." CNN reported that 168 people were killed, calling it "the largest terrorist attack on U.S. soil," and the public was out for blood. But when it was discovered that Timothy McVeigh and his accomplices were white, the sense of outrage was transformed, almost overnight, into a more muted anger, a specific

---

2. Vandana Shiva, "Terrorism as Cannibalism," *ZNet Daily Commentaries*, 23 January 2002.

3. Juan Gonzalez, "Grieving Voice Pleads for Peace," *New York Daily News*, 19 September 2001.

criminal trial against a specific white person. When it was discovered that Timothy McVeigh was a right-wing ideologue who blew up the building because he hated the federal government, a symbol of civil rights and Black equality, who had been trained by the U.S. army to use explosives, there was no effort to connect him to the broader white racist movement. There was no national campaign against right-wing hate groups.[4] How was that possible? Because Bill Clinton, president at the time, had been elected by a margin of white good old boys. Because the Republican Party saw the violence as an extension of its own right-wing politics and saw McVeigh and the vigilantes, just like the bombers and murderers at abortion clinics, as useful if somewhat overzealous members of their own united front.

As we wake up to the threat of the Bush execution of this war against the world, we can recognize that it is fundamentally an extension of the policy of world domination that already existed on September 10, or on September 2 in Durban when the U.S. government walked out of WCAR. Obviously, the September 11 events give even greater advantage to the Bush Administration's specific tactical plan for internal governance of the "homeland" and external conquest of the world. A look at

---

4. On July 24, 2002, William Pierce, the author of *The Turner Diaries* and founder of the Right-wing National Alliance, died of cancer at the age of 68. In his short obituary on the web, it explained that *The Turner Diaries*, written under the pen name Andrew Macdonald and published in 1978, depicts a violent overthrow of the government by a small band of white supremacists who finance themselves through counterfeiting and bank robbery. Set at the end of the 20th century, it describes a fictional truck bombing of FBI headquarters in Washington, DC—a scene that roughly prefigures the Oklahoma City bombing. *It has long been standard reading among supremacist and extremist groups and gained notoriety as a book favored by Oklahoma City bomber Timothy McVeigh. (Associated Press Newswire*, July 24, 2002).

the Bush/Cheney tactical plan for the imperialist world order will help shape our own post-Durban movement of resistance. Their extreme push to the Right is frightening, but it offers the potential for a broad antiracist, anti-war, anti-imperialist resistance, that can build a broad united front for democratic rights and non-intervention by the U.S. government. This is a chance for a reconstruction of a U.S. Left, if it is capable of providing some leadership.

The Bush/Right Wing Organizing Plan: Theocracy in the White House

The Bush/Cheney plan begins with an aggressive push for U.S. control over the world's resources, with particular emphasis on oil, and the consolidation of the home front in support of empire. Its approach is ideologically tied to the hard line religious Right, a virulent anticommunist free market crusade, and a warmongering based on U.S. chauvinism and ultra-patriotism. Significant sectors of the "public," and especially the majority of the white electorate, buy into a massive repetition of the national myth that the U.S. is always the victim, never the aggressor, but fights back with a vengeance. This theocratic view of the U.S. as uniquely blessed—"God bless America"—is rooted in a strong electoral bloc of white, male, Christian "Bible Belt" racists for whom constant retribution against communists, terrorists, and other heathens or nonbelievers is the manifest destiny of the United States. This is reinforced by awareness that the domination of the world is not just good for big business but has been the material basis of the high standard of living for the white middle and working classes in particular. Some of these benefits eventually trickle down to many in the working classes of peoples of color, who, even in their severe oppression and exploitation inside the U.S., benefit from the relative strength of the U.S. economy over all Third World nations.

The recent Supreme Court ruling upholding public subsidies of religious school education, so-called "school vouchers," and the orchestrated national hysteria against a U.S. Ninth Circuit judge who correctly ruled that the insertion of "Under God" in the "Pledge of Allegiance" was unconstitutional reflect massive victories for the religious Right whose influence begins with President Bush and Supreme Court Justice Antonin Scalia and proclaims a holy war against Godless infidels at home and abroad.[5]

The United States has evolved out of the anti-monarchy struggle of white, male, property-owning capitalists who were slavers, pirates, and mass murderers of Indigenous peoples. Many of the settlers, and the U.S., like South Africa, is a white settler state, were also religious fanatics. Their fight with the British crown was purely tactical. They did not like the terms of the colonial deal and their democratic rhetoric of revolution was hypocritical. Still, they constructed a constitution based on a secular model that tried to protect free market capitalism from the encroachment of royalty and church—thus the once-vaunted "separation of church and state." The colonists always used their religious freedom selectively, claiming God's will to justify white supremacy, slavery, and the conquest of Mexico, Hawaii, Cuba,

---

5. Sean Wilentz, "From Justice Scalia, a Chilling Vision of Religion's Authority in America," *New York Times*, 8 July 2002.

the Philippines and all of "the Americas," while imposing Christianity on the surviving Indian tribes they did not wipe out altogether. As with all U.S. freedoms, the freedom from church interference in the secular state was only a white, property-owning man's freedom. Still, the "separation of church and state" served the system well for centuries.

The last 20 years of victories by the religious Right threaten secular democratic rights, while the rise of ideological fanatics to all levels of government creates a series of contradictions for the system. Large numbers of people, from civil libertarians to moderate Christians to Jews, Muslims, atheists and agnostics, to anyone who believes that society should be based on secular principles, is in potential opposition. Any time a system draws a hard line in the sand, it forces others into opposition, or at least potential opposition. The abuses of the Church, its long history of colonial occupation, racial discrimination, avarice, fire and brimstone hypocrisy, and financial and sexual abuse are well known. An antiracist Left has the opportunity to lead a broad united front and an aggressive campaign against the religious Right and its warmongering move toward Armageddon.

The Reversal of Democratic Rights at Home

During the war in Vietnam, the U.S. experimented with a complex strategy of genocide abroad and expanded civil rights and civil liberties at home. This was based on a ruling class strategy reflected in Lyndon Johnson's administration that it could not fight two wars at the same time. That is, there was an effort to "integrate" the Civil Rights Movement into the system while violating the Nuremberg statutes in Vietnam. (The infiltration of left groups by the COINTELPRO program and the imprisonment and murder of Black revolutionaries does not contradict this overall trend—this is still capitalism). The system's overextension in fact helped both the Black Liberation Movement and the Vietnamese revolution, for in still trying to fight on two fronts the system lost both wars. It was a lesson that supports the general theory of Che Guevara "Create Two, Three Many Vietnams."

Out of the many ruling class sum-ups of their mistakes during the Vietnam War period, one faction argued that the capitalist press gave far too much media attention to the realities of war and the opposition of social movements and the government and police gave far too much latitude to protest. The massive consolidation of media monopolies—typified by right-wing Rupert Murdoch's international media empire Newscorp (how fitting, a "news corporation"), coupled with the right-wing control of virtually every "talk radio" outlet, has created even more mechanisms for the Big Lie to be disseminated. This includes the unspoken but quite evident policy of censoring coverage of most anti-system protests.[6] I will not elaborate what should be obvious, that the Patriot Act and the formation of a Department of Homeland Security are creations that only a few decades ago even the most rabid Right-Winger would dismiss as hopeful fantasy, but that are now qualitative expansions of 20 years of the most virulent attacks on civil liberties. What is the goal? To create a permanent national security state whose main target is a future U.S. left opposition, or any counterhegemonic voice for that matter, dissenting from the permanent war state.

---

6. See the excellent work of Fairness and Accuracy in Reporting, FAIR, available from www.fair.org.

The Right Wing supports the police state by inflaming an already predisposed public that only those who "commit crimes" or plan to subvert the government need fear the loss of their constitutional and human rights. The relationship between racism and a right-wing police state is clear—for most whites, "crime" is code for the actions of Blacks, as virtually every move Black people have tried to make in this country has been ruled "illegal" from the outset—even their so-called "right" to get out of slavery. Television today is flooded with police shows. They portray mainly Black and Latino "criminals" getting out of doing time because of public defenders. Recently, when O.J. Simpson exercised his constitutional rights and was acquitted, a mass hysteria developed over a Black lawyer, Johnny Cochran, who was charged by his white fellow defense attorney of "playing the race card." Cochran's crime? Raising the idea with a jury that a white racist policeman might plant evidence to obtain a conviction against a Black man. The long-held view, that this country could have "democratic rights" for whites and fascism and genocide for everyone else, which was momentarily reversed by the victories of the New Left, is at the core of the reconstruction of an explicitly repressive criminal justice system.

Julian Bond, the 1960s Student Non-violent Coordinating Committee (SNCC) activist, now the Chairman of the Board of the NAACP, has warned about "a right-wing conspiracy operating out of the U.S. Department of Justice."[7] Calling the attorney general "J. Edgar Ashcroft," he warned about the re-establish-

---

7. Lori Rodriguez, "Bond Opens Up NAACP Conference With Swipe at Bush 'Dynasty,'" *Houston Chronicle*, 8 July 2002.

ment of a COINTELPRO counterinsurgency program to infiltrate antiracist and anti-war groups, using the tactics of "spies and lies." It will take, again, the Black-led Civil Rights Movement or a new incarnation of it, to link the fights for racial justice and against empire to demands for the fullest rights of speech, assembly, and protest.

The Reversal of Civil Rights Remedies— The Sandoval Case

It has been so long since there has been a vibrant civil rights movement that every reversal of civil rights law and policy is met with little more than muted protest by what remains of the civil rights establishment. On April 24, 2001, the U.S. Supreme Court, in another Scalia-led attack, ruled by its usual 5 to 4 majority in *Alexander v. Sandoval* to fatally weaken one of the key provisions of the 1964 Civil Rights Act. Title VI of the act states, "No person in the United States shall, on the ground of race, color, or national origin, be excluded from participation in, be denied the benefits of, or be subjected to discrimination under any program or activity receiving federal financial assistance." Moreover, it allows private parties, that is, civil rights groups, individuals and groups suffering racial discrimination, to bring individual or class action suits. The penalty for states or cities is profound—the loss of all federal funds in programs proven to be discriminatory.

Our own organizations, the Labor/Community Strategy Center and the Bus Riders Union, in 1994, brought a class action lawsuit under Title VI, *Labor/Community Strategy Center and Bus Riders Union, et al. v. Los Angeles Metropolitan*

Transportation Authority (MTA), represented by the NAACP Legal Defense and Educational Fund (LDF). We charged the MTA with creating a separate and unequal mass transportation system that discriminated against 400,000 daily bus riders, almost 90 percent of whom are Black, Latino, and Asian/Pacific Islander.[8] This led to a negotiated consent decree in which the MTA agreed to lower bus fares and to fund a massive modernization and expansion of the bus fleet. After eight years of continued legal argument and sustained pressure by our vibrant grassroots movement, the MTA lowered bus fares, retired 2,200 dilapidated diesel buses, and purchased 2,200 clean fuel compressed natural gas buses, moving more than one billion dollars in public funds to the bus system (and to low-income Black, Latino, Asian Pacific Islander, and white bus riders). This is the power of the Civil Rights Act and Title VI when placed in the hands of a dynamic, militant civil rights organization.

Unfortunately, because Title VI is one of the last legal and constitutional weapons of a declining civil rights movement, the Scalia/Clarence Thomas faction were able to impose their view in *Alexander v. Sandoval* that the last 35 years of civil rights history had to be overturned. Private parties, according to this ideological perspective, could no longer bring class action suits on racism under Title VI unless they could prove "intentional discrimination," a very difficult legal standard. Therefore, if the racial discrimination lawsuit is based on "disparate impact," that is, if plaintiffs can prove massive racial disparities in the pro-

8. The Korean Immigrant Workers Advocates (KIWA) and the Southern Christian Leadership Conference (SCLC) joined the Strategy Center and BRU as organizational plaintiffs, while BRU members Pearl Daniels, Maria Guardado, Noemi Zelada, and Ricardo Zelada were named plaintiffs.

vision of governmental services or programs, but cannot prove intentional discrimination to the satisfaction of a (right-wing) judge, then they can no longer bring such suits. Under *Sandoval* only the U.S. attorney general, in this case John Ashcroft, has the legal right to bring the suit (a legal option that combines Catch 22 with the Twilight Zone.) But, where is the outcry from the civil rights establishment or Jesse Jackson or the Congressional Black Caucus? Unlike the way the National Rifle Association goes ballistic if they are denied the right to have a howitzer in every home, there has been a profound silence on *Alexander v. Sandoval.* Another major weapon that people fought and died for over centuries is being taken away from an already beleaguered and disoriented civil rights movement without a whine or a whimper.

The Bush Administration and the accommodating Democrats are making a major strategic reversal of a ruling class strategy to "integrate" people of color in general and Black people in particular into a traditionally white racist society. The system cannot sustain the reform of civil rights. The "white backlash" began almost from the first day of the Civil Rights Movement, and neither of the white Southern good old boys Bush or Gore chose to run on an antiracist platform (nor did Ralph Nader). The reversal of Title VI and of much of the 1964 Civil Rights Act reopens the wounds of structural racism at home, and leaves Blacks, Latinos, and Asian/Pacific Islanders with dramatically reduced legal avenues to challenge the most grotesque policies of racial discrimination. What ever happened to Dr. King's dream? If the U.S. puts two million people in jail, more than 60 percent of whom are Black and Latino, sends Blacks and Latinos to the electric chair en masse, and cuts housing, schools and hospitals in ways to demolish the lives of people of color, as long as it does so in a way that oppresses some white people as well, and as long as it does not hang out a sign saying "We do this intentionally, we are racists," then the *Sandoval* decision dramatically reduces the right to even bring a case, let alone win it.

The capitulation of the civil rights establishment with its new fascination with Black, Latino, and Asian capitalism, is a major setback to a broad united front for democratic rights, and the struggle with those forces cannot be abandoned. Still, it creates an enormous opening for an antiracist Left. In fact, there is no chance of rebuilding such a broad united front on civil rights unless there is new leadership from a more militant, anticapitalist, working class-led antiracist movement. Learning from history, during the 1960s. a new group of militant, antiracist organizations—the Congress of Racial Equality (CORE), Student Non-violent Coordinating Committee (SNCC), Northern Student Movement, tendencies within the Southern Christian Leadership Conference (SCLC), and later, the Black Panthers, led a revolution within the Civil Rights Movement. They challenged the conservative, tied-to-the-Democratic-Party civil rights establishment of the NAACP and Urban League as well as much of the Black church establishment. They were able to simultaneously build a broad antiracist united front and push it to the left. Today, that challenge falls to many of the antiracist groups participating in the People of Color Environmental Justice Leadership Summit and many of the U.S. antiracist groups that participated in Durban.[9] As of now, there is no viable coordinated

9. First National People of Color Environmental Leadership Summit took place in Washington, DC in 1991.

movement, no alliance of Blacks, Latinos, Asian/Pacific Islanders and antiracist whites, in any combination, to fill this political
vacuum, and there is no guarantee it will be filled. But the system is making a very bold gamble. If, for example, the
Reparations Movement gets off the ground, the reversal of civil
rights could be just the historical jumpstart for a new antiracist
politics and a new antiracist movement.

The Effort to "Integrate" Blacks and Latinos into a Patriotic, Pro-imperialist Bloc

George W. Bush, aware of the absence of a viable and militant
Black or Latino mass Left, and aware that the Democrats want
to cultivate "minority" voters without fighting for minority rights,
has moved strategically to cut away the Democratic Party's last
remaining electoral stronghold—the Black and Latino vote. While
many parodied the pathetic Republican multicultural stage show
at its virtually all-white nominating convention, in fact Bush has
moved to cultivate a Black and Latino conservative leadership.
While gutting the civil rights of the majority, Bush is integrating
a few people of color into leadership, knowing that Black and
Latino communities have more difficulty fighting for their rights
when the people violating them look like them. There is no question that the elevation of Colin Powell and Condoleezza Rice to
positions of authority in the Republican administration has contributed to disorientation in the Black community in particular
about its response to Bush's imperial ambitions.

    In our organizing work in Los Angeles, we have seen a ter-
rible regression into a self-interested and often reactionary
politics among many Black and Latino elected officials, church

leaders and college faculty who not only have refused to support the civil rights demands of the Bus Riders Union, but worse, have become members of the voracious government contract-grubbing comprador elite. In our civil rights lawsuit, MTA CEO Franklin White and MTA Board member Yvonne Brathwaite Burke, who are Black, and County Supervisor Gloria Molina and City Councilman Richard Alatorre, Latino board members, were defendants. The federal courts, in issuing a temporary restraining order against the MTA, agreed that MTA policies were violating the civil rights of 400,000 overwhelmingly Latino and Black bus riders. The creation of larger and larger layers of Black, Latino, and Asian/Pacific Islander elites who are directly involved in the suppression of their own people—the formalization of what Franz Fanon and Mao Tse Tung referred to as a "comprador bourgeoisie" directly tied to imperialism—is a brilliant tactical plan by the establishment. The danger for this bourgeoisie is that it forces the Black, Latino and Asian/Pacific Islander working classes to develop their own independent left politics or die under a facile multiracialism and co-optive multiculturalism that suppresses both their class and national interests.

Again, there is little formalized rebellion as of yet, little self-consciously formulated working class-led antiracist politics that would root the struggle in a structural analysis of national oppression, seek out allies of all races, including the critical constituency of antiracist whites, that would reject superficial and narrow nationalism and seek out anticolonial allies throughout the world. Bush and the Democrats are betting that will not happen. But the fight against the comprador bourgeoisie and the assertion of its own independent class interests in the national and class struggles is the historical responsibility of the working class of color—the basis of an independent left politics of antagonism to both major parties.

Deregulated Capitalism: The Danger of False Prophets and False Profits

Obviously capitalism has shown an enormous resiliency and staying power. Over the years, I have based my politics on a vision of a capitalist system falling apart politically more than economically. Still, the present period is truly revolutionary as we begin to witness the most profound disintegration of imperialism's vaunted economic system and see the seeds of its permanent instability and crisis. As part of a collective writing project that produced *Toward a Program of Resistance*, we have put forth the analysis that imperialism is capitalism in its moribund stage, with a tendency towards parasitic and speculative investments, the super-exploitation of oppressed nations and colonies to prop up the "home" market, and an inexorable drive toward world war to constantly redivide the world market in each imperialist nation's interest.[10]

The stock market bubble of the 1990s—the singular contribution of Clinton/Gore, "it's the economy stupid," Democratic electoral victories—has turned out to be one of the all-time frauds. Its structural excess has gone well beyond the market

---

10. Program Demand Group, *Toward a Program of Resistance* (Los Angeles: An AhoraNow Commentary, 2002). The original presentation of this analysis of monopoly capitalism as imperialism can be found in V.I. Lenin, *Imperialism: The Highest Stage of Capitalism* (London: Junius Pub., 1996).

"bubble" first imagined into the "casino capitalism" about which Fidel Castro has tried to warn the world. Clinton/Gore came to power on a carefully constructed Democratic Leadership Council strategy to move the Democratic Party to the right, to force the Democratic liberals into acquiescence: "You've lost every presidential election; you've got no place to go." Clinton came to power by stealing many Republican themes, including an unabashedly pro-business program to deregulate the capitalist markets and undermine the New Deal reforms that tried to regulate out-of-control capitalism in the best long term interests of capitalism.

A frenzied "Bull" stock market based on constantly growing and escalating "growth stocks" of technology companies has turned out to be way beyond a stock market "bubble." It proved and is still proving, to be a capitalist house of cards. Desperate companies—Enron, Tyco, WorldCom, Global Crossing, Xerox, and the list keeps growing—have routinely overstated profits and covered up massive losses. These stocks were talked up by analysts and stock brokers from investment banks that were financing the fraud and then further covered up by large accounting firms such as Arthur Andersen that were paid as consultants to cook the books. CEOs voted themselves stock options that were not reported as expenses, again inflating profits, and when the end was near, cashed out their stock options shortly before the stock of their own companies cratered.

This was the culmination of 20 years of neoliberal deregulation, with crisis after crisis, from Savings and Loans to Enron. In essence, capitalism moved from a ruthless system of the production and sale of real goods to a speculative frenzy in which many companies had no products to sell at all and others simply used the alchemist's trick of turning base metals into gold. For a decade, TV business shows abounded, and assembly line workers and even clerks at Office Depot and Wal-Mart became overnight stock market gurus, only to see their life savings and speculative gains evaporate in front of their eyes.[11]

As public outcry has become shrill and hysterical—after all, almost everyone who lost money, even at the bottom, was a willing player in the Ponzi scheme—the Bush Administration is doing a bad imitation of outrage, while offering the most superficial reforms that will have little effect. Bush argues that his reforms will protect successful capitalism from the few bad apples, but what if the problem is the speculative and unstable nature of capitalism itself?

In the midst of the faux reform is another round of the U.S. capitalist state subsidizing businesses that cannot make profits without the government literally manufacturing them—big government bailing out big business through corporate welfare. As Bush lectures the poor on "self-reliance," he approved a bipartisan binge for U.S. agribusiness, $51 billion in additional federal subsidies over the next six years. As housing and hospitals and schools disintegrate, the government can find a billion dollars for the airline industry and billions for the agribusiness industry. The system is imploding but is basing its economic strategy on profits at any price. Bush assumes that the war hysteria and patriotic posturing will continue to keep the white electorate and a growing conservative core of people of color seeing the protection of the empire as their central class interest, no matter what the personal costs. But what if this calculation backfires?

---

11. Vijay Prashad writes in detail about this deregulation in *Fat Cats and Running Dogs: The Enron Stage of Capitalism* (Monroe, Maine: Common Courage Press, 2002).

The core of this capitalist crisis is that U.S. corporations have come to depend upon fraudulent statements of profits because their actual profits are declining or even nonexistent. This crisis of declining profits leads to a further exploitation of the world. This drives the system toward world wars, reflected in the effort to control Iraq's oil supplies and the further exploitation and super-exploitation of the colonies. This merciless squeezing of Third World nations was reflected in the ruthless Doha and Monterrey rounds of World Trade Organization negotiations in which the U.S. and EU bullied them into even further subjugation against their national interests. The drive to further exploit the earth's resources with no regard for ecological viability is reflected in the Bush Administration's refusal to sign the Kyoto treaty on global warming and its demands for new opportunities for oil drilling throughout the world. Again, its risky business to prop up an inherently unstable system.

Structural Adjustment at Home:
The Racist Dismantling of the Welfare State

As the stock market continues to unravel, going back to the levels of 1997, most of the people who made money during the "Bull market" (1982-2000) have now lost all of their gains and many have lost much of their original savings. The much vaunted, "who needs that damn social security when you can have the 'freedom' to invest it in the capitalist stock market" talk is out of fashion—how fast capitalist booms can turn into busts. Still, the question is, will people cry in their beer, fight each other, or fight the system?

During the 1930s Depression, at the height of communist influence in the U.S. labor movement and growing socialist and communist influence throughout Europe and what would later be called "the Third World," Franklin Delano Roosevelt built a united front of progressive capitalists terrified that their cohorts' unchecked greed would bring down the whole house of cards. White workers were in a militant, populist mood and demanded some protections from the worst vicissitudes of the capitalist market—thus the drive for unemployment insurance and social security. But even at the height of left influence, these reform demands were terribly modest because of the scourge of racism that has always limited the vision and resolve of white workers—even to the point of sabotaging their own narrow class interests. Even worse, white racism in the working class led to the exclusion of Latino, Filipino, and Black farm workers and sharecroppers from the National Labor Relations Act, which exempted the farm industry, and as such, most agricultural workers of color.[12] The FDR strategy did stabilize the system, as the white workers during the 1930s were still so dominant politically within the working class electorate that the New Deal reforms met their basic demands. For Black and Latino workers during the 1930s and W.W.II, their struggle did not yet reach revolutionary capacity or impact and was not able to shake the dominant white racism of the white workers. Still, the strange fruit of southern lynchings and the bitter fruit of the FDR betrayal set the conditions for an expansion of Black radicalism.

---

12. The economic populism did not apply to Black workers who were denied access to white industry; as such, the Roosevelt Administration consistently rejected anti-discrimination laws and anti-lynching laws as many white workers preferred to murder, or watch the murder of, Blacks than fight in a multiracial antiracist class alliance.

During the 1960s, visionary thinkers like George Wylie, formerly from CORE, helped to organize the National Welfare Rights Organization (NWRO) along with many black women from the ranks of welfare recipients such as NWRO President Johnnie Tillmon and Marion Kidd, who began her organizing with the Newark Community Union Project. Fannie Lou Hamer and Victoria Gray organized sharecroppers and poor farmers in Mississippi into SNCC and the Mississippi Freedom Democratic Party. Martin Luther King moved from the fight for civil rights and desegregation to initiate a poor people's campaign. They began to theorize the need for a Black-led movement of all low-income working people, including poor whites. These movements won the first significant changes in social welfare legislation since the 1930s, focusing on the needs of the unemployed, women, and the urban and rural poor. Ironically, their efforts benefited the white poor the most, even though most of the grassroots leaders were Black women.

But by 1980, Ronald Reagan's appeal to "Reagan Democrats" was code for the attack on Black people and an appeal to the chauvinism of white workers, which reporters even today code as "socially conservative." Many white male workers hated the welfare state, believed in Christian self-reliance based on the theft of property from Indigenous peoples and the enslavement of Blacks, and harbored a hatred of Blacks, women, and especially Black women. As such, Reagan's abusive attacks on "welfare queens" struck a responsive note and began the free fall, one incremental step at a time, of the social welfare state that FDR, Lyndon Johnson, and yes, at times, Richard Nixon had constructed.

It is hard to imagine how Bush's "compassionate conservative" strategy can work. It is hard to describe how unbearable things have become for the Black, Latino, and Asian/Pacific Islander working class, the immigrant working class, and for many white workers, employed and unemployed, as well. Just one example: L.A. County, one of the richest areas in the world and, like every county in the U.S., a recipient of federal funds, just announced the closing of one hospital and more than ten neighborhood clinics, the latest in an avalanche of medical service cuts over the last decade. The decision was made by the five L.A. County Supervisors, Mike Antonovich, Zev Yaroslavsky, Gloria Molina, Yvonne Brathwaite Burke, and Don Knabe, who preside over one of the most undemocratic electoral systems in the U.S. where there are only five electoral districts for ten million people. When challenged about the cuts, conservative Republican Antonovich commented, "Well, we can't have a hospital on every corner." This at a time when people are dying on their way to county hospitals and there are no hospitals for miles and miles, let alone one on every corner. These recent attacks fall most heavily on the urban and rural working class of color and are truly heartbreaking. They also hurt the white poor, working class, and middle class, but their historical refusal to fight for government "social welfare" services and unwillingness to ally with Blacks and Latinos make a unified "class" struggle impossible.

Every time Teddy Kennedy holds a hearing on medical services or insurance or corporate fraud, poor white people come out of the woodwork to complain about the loss of their livelihoods, but most of them wouldn't be caught dead at a World Conference Against Racism, where the only real hope for reversing the attacks on welfare would reside. Over the centuries, poor whites have made their peace with the system, and Bush continues to punish them for their conciliation. Ironically, it is still far-sighted Leftists, many of whom are organizers of color, who do not want to write off the possibility, no matter how remote, of multiracial alliances with the larger sectors of the white working class.

As the Bush Administration continues to amass massive budget deficits to fight a war that changes targets daily, it continues to raid already depleted social programs for giveaways to transnational corporations. The Republicans in Congress, not satisfied with the blood they are already extracting from welfare recipients, are trying to raise the work requirement from 30 hours a week to 40. The kinder and gentler Democrats are pointing out that it is far more difficult for women to get childcare under those more onerous conditions. Still, Bush cleverly announces he will veto any efforts to go back on Bill Clinton's plan to force the poor to work—or else. How far we have fallen when 30 versus 40 hours of forced labor for the poor sets the parameters of the two-party debate.

Mass rebellions and revolts must begin with objective conditions. Social movements, radical grassroots organizations, and eventually, an organized and coordinated Left do not automatically sink roots in the soil of oppression, but that is where they must begin. Project South in Atlanta sees the growing emiseration of poor whites as providing at least a chance to build the long-dreamed-of alliance of Black and white workers. At the same time, they stress the need for political education against capitalism and white supremacy, as well as Black leadership, if such an essential experiment has a chance to succeed. In every Black, Latino and Asian/Pacific Islander community there are dedicated groups fighting the daily attacks. People Organized to Win Employment Rights (POWER) in San Francisco, the Center for Third World Organizing in Oakland, and the National Campaign for Jobs and Income Support are just a few examples of groups trying to build a movement against "welfare deform."

Bush is again taking a calculated gamble that replicates on the domestic terrain the structural adjustment programs imposed on Third World nations. In so doing, he makes the anti-imperialist Left's call for a strategic alliance between oppressed peoples in the U.S. and the Third World rooted in an even greater material reality, and creates the conditions for a world wide fight against neoliberalism.

Attacks on Immigrants: Social Chauvinism Back in the Driver's Seat

In a wave that reached a crest after the victories and then relative quiescence of the civil rights movements, resentment against and attacks upon Latino and Asian/Pacific Islander immigrants were rife during the 1980s and 1990s. The national crescendo may have been reached during California's 1994 Proposition 187 anti-immigrant campaign, in which conservative California Governor Pete Wilson rode to re-election on the heels of a ballot initiative to deprive undocumented immigrants of any government programs, even food and medical care. Worse, the racist white majority electorate passed this draconian measure—too many whites see no connection between their European immigrant experience and the suffering of Mexican and Asian immigrants. A growing Black conservative electorate, threatened by immigrant labor, feeling and being politically disenfranchised, competing with

Latinos for political power and the spoils of empire, also bought into a racist appeal that linked them with the white majority as "real Americans"—just as Latinos often bond with whites against Blacks in these Byzantine racial power plays in which it is always the whites who benefit from divisions among people of color. But the anti-immigrant attack backfired on the Republicans, as a Latino Left led a very militant and nationalist opposition to Proposition 187. They defied conservative ideology by marching with the Mexican flag, and many conservative Latinos bolted to the Democratic Party in California, as even the documented immigrants and Latino citizens understood the threat to their livelihoods and cultures.[13]

When George Bush evolved his political strategy in Texas, watching what the Republicans summed up as the excesses of the Pete Wilson tactics, he decided to cultivate the Latino elite and press them for delivery of the votes of their ethnic constituency that he needed to be elected governor. This coincided with a change of tactics by the AFL-CIO leadershp that went from being virulently anti-immigrant to welcoming the rise of Justice for Janitors (Service Employees International Union, SEIU) and other predominantly Latino unions in California as they realized

---

13. UPDATE on Prop 187 from the American Civil Liberties Union (ACLU): In March 1998, U.S. District Judge Mariana Pfaelzer issued a final ruling in the ACLU's challenge to Proposition 187, confirming the federal government's exclusive authority over immigration and declaring the measure unconstitutional. A court-approved mediation on July 29, 1999 ended years of legal and political debate over Proposition 187, validating the 1998 ruling to overturn the proposition. See "Judge Rules Prop. 187 Unconstitutional, States May Not Make Own Immigration Laws," *ACLU News*, vol. LXII, no. 4 (Jan/Feb 1998). The recent Bush Administration effort to place new attacks on immigrants in the federal Department of Justice circumvents this ruling, by exercising the "federal government's exclusive authority." Other political and constitutional challenges will be needed.

they were losing "native" members hand over fist. Similarly, many capitalists relied on immigrants as a source of low-wage labor. But as the system tried to stabilize its "immigrant problem," trying to quiet down the white majority while quietly cultivating Latinos and the super pro-capitalist Mexican president Vicente Fox, the new war against the world has reopened the anti-immigrant epidemic, rounding up Arabs and Muslims by the thousands, and placing all immigrants in one Immigration and Naturalization Service net.

The *Los Angeles Times* recently reported:

> The Justice Department announced that it would require all noncitizens to report changes of address within 10 days of moving or risk financial penalties, jail, and even deportation. The plan, which is based on a long neglected 50-year-old law, would apply to 10 million people who are living in the United States legally, but not as American citizens. More than 1 million are estimated to live in Los Angeles County alone. The new plan also covers illegal immigrants—said to number 8 to 9 million people nationally—but few are expected to step forward.[14]

As the Justice Department now singles out 18 to 19 million immigrants nationally and has eliminated the separation between the local police and the INS, the dragnet around more and more of the population begins. Significantly, since September 11, six thousand Arab and Muslim men have been rounded up and imprisoned without being charged. Still, many immigrant rights

---

14. Jonathan Peterson, "Noncitizens Must Report If They Move," *Los Angeles Times*, 23 July 2002.

groups are in fact, quite conservative, as some groups formerly headed by immigrant Leftists have now turned to safe messages and corporate sponsorship. Similarly, in the summer of 2002, the influential American-Arab Anti-Discrimination Committee (ADC) that has done important advocacy work around issues of racial profiling of Arabs since September 11, fired its extremely popular Western Regional director, Michel Shehadeh, for his aggressive support of the Palestinian struggle and his willingness to challenge the Bush Administration, which the more conservative board members wanted to cultivate. The debate about the politics of immigrant rights—fighting for nondiscrimination inside the empire or simultaneously fighting for democratic rights and challenging the broader objectives of the empire—will shape the possibilities of future resistance as the Bush Administration again expands the scope of its repression and the size of a potential opposition.

The Empire Strikes and Strikes Back: The Recolonization and Emiseration of the Third World

During 40 years of post-World War II anticolonial upsurge, many Third World nations experimented for the first time in centuries with pro-socialist self-government. In the past 20 years, however, a world wide movement of neoliberal reaction led by the United States and Britain (beginning with Reagan and Thatcher) has overthrown many of the left and progressive governments in the Third World and replaced them with a neoliberal "free market" approach buttressed by military and political dictatorships to suppress popular opposition. As one example, the U.S.-backed overthrow and murder of the popularly elected Salvador Allende and the crimes of Augosto Pinochet's military regime were essential to the neoliberal model in Chile. One frightening trend of the past 20 years is the recolonization of many nations, in which the "privatization" of public assets involves wealthy transnationals stealing the public resources of Third World nations. This has destroyed the economic base of those nations, reimposed debt burdens, and placed the cost of most social services outside the boundaries of the impoverished masses or their governments. The U.S., through its worldwide economic dictatorship—the International Monetary Fund, World Bank, and World Trade Organization— has created an increasingly integrated world economic system in which any Third World nations' demands for self-determination or efforts to extricate themselves from the imperialist economic web are increasingly off limits. Recent international conferences on the economy in Doha, Qatar and Monterrey, Mexico have tightened the noose even further, over the furious but so far unsuccessful protests of nations in the Global South.

At both the World Conference Against Racism and the PrepComs for the World Summit on Sustainable Development, nations of the Global South are protesting the privatization of their own forests, mines, water, and sanitation services. They are asserting that access to water, food, and medicine is a human right and demanding that natural resources be developed in environmentally sustainable ways that benefit their own nations, not foreign, predatory investors.

Ecological catastrophe

The devastating ecological impact of Western capitalist models of development has led groups in the Third World (and communities of color in the U.S) to critique "environmental racism," and demand "ecological debt" from the West as part of the antiracist, anti-imperialist program of broader reparations. Global warming and climate change have led to massive ocean floods of the Small Island States. The new term in ecological parlance, "extreme weather events," caused by greenhouse gases and climate change, refers to the droughts, floods, hurricanes, and tornadoes that are taking place at a scale and a frequency that are off the charts of centuries of recorded natural occurrences—again, they are most severe in the nations of Asia, Africa, and Latin America.

At the Rio conference in 1992 (the UN Conference on Environment and Development, UNCED), the world governments adopted the principle of "common but differentiated responsibilities." This meant that all nations had responsibility for the ecological crisis; but since the Western governments had caused the most damage, they had the most responsibility to change their policies. For example, the United States alone is the largest single contributor to greenhouse gas emissions, producing 25 percent of the world's emissions, while all the 130 developing nations together produce 24 percent. It is the unsustainable production and consumption patterns in the U.S., the EU, and increasingly, the more advanced capitalist countries in the Global South (such as Malaysia, Singapore, Korea, Taiwan, China, Brazil, Venezuela, and Mexico) that are threatening the existence of many

Third World nations and the world.[15] In 1992, the response by a defiant U.S. president George Bush, Sr. was that "the world cannot tell the people in the United States to change our lifestyle." Ten years later, another George Bush is escalating ecological defiance. He is simultaneously denying that global warming is caused by "man made" actions and arguing that, even if it is, it's too late to do anything about it. Even with the true wonder of millions of years of evolution in danger of extinction, the capitalist mantra is "more, more, more" and the September 11 events are being used to legitimize and even exceed the death-defying political economy of imperialism.

At WCAR, the Environmental Justice caucus, whose roots are in many Black, Latino, Asian/Pacific Islander, and Indigenous communities in the U.S., took a more proactive internationalist stand, linking up with South African activists and writing strong language in the NGO Programme of Action. Many of the EJ caucus members will also be present at Johannesburg at the WSSD to challenge the "lifestyle" of the Bush Administration.

Suppression of Self-determination and Revolutionary Activity

It should be obvious that for much of the world and certainly for much of the Third World, there is an urgent need for revolutionary alternatives to the growing vice of U.S.-dominated economic, political, and ecological development. On their own,

---

15. California Environmental Protection Agency, "U.S. Is the Largest Single Contributor to Greenhouse Gas Emissions," *AB1493 (Pavley) Briefing Package: Global Warming and Greenhouse Gas Emissions from Motor Vehicles*, PowerPoint presentation, 24 July 2002.

the world revolutionary forces are generally weak, and in each nation, movements for self-determination would of course be built on determining the best form of government, the best form of economy, and the urgently needed independence to even contemplate a non-capitalist future. And yet, even more daunting than the present conditions of poverty, epidemic, extreme weather events, and foreign domination is the completely understood reality that any effort to extricate oneself from the worldwide web of imperialist domination will lead to U.S. intervention and counter-revolution. In South Africa, those who demand a challenge to neoliberalism, as well as those who defend it, openly discuss the threat to South Africa's sovereignty of a CIA-sponsored counter-revolution. (I am well aware that some Third World Nations, such as the People's Republic of China, that have significant military and political leverage to fight off U.S. power, have voluntarily adopted many ecologically destructive policies of their own.)

Since September 11, the U.S. has actively participated in a coup d'etat against the elected government of President Hugo Chavez in Venezuela, who fortunately was able to beat back an April 2002 military takeover. The U.S. has also openly announced its plan to remove Saddam Hussein from power in Iraq, has told the Palestinian people that they must get rid of Yasir Arafat, and is expanding military aid to Colombia to try to destroy the popular revolutionary movement in the countryside led by the FARC-EP (Revolutionary Armed Forces of Colombia-People's Army). According to the Bush Doctrine, armed peasants fighting the oil giants in Burma, resistance movements in the Philippines, and all peoples fighting against starvation and misery are now targeted as part of a ubiquitous enemy.

In response, the U.S. Left has to prioritize the defense of the Right to Revolution in the Third World in particular and a call for no U.S. intervention in the internal affairs of other nations.

The Institutionalization of the U.S. as a Military Behemoth and Permanent Aggressor

The liberals and the Left have always complained about what Eisenhower labeled "the military industrial complex," but year after year the U.S. Pentagon and military budget have eaten a larger and larger piece of the Gross Domestic Product and the national budget. Almost beyond belief, the annual U.S. military budget is now $396 billion, almost ten times those of Russia, China, and Japan, and almost 20 times that of Germany.[16] Most often, the liberals have tried to argue that "overspending" on "defense" has stolen from urgent social programs, and that many of the U.S. weapons represent "overkill" with an implied imperialist view that killing is fine, it's just that overkill is redundant and wasteful. The U.S. Pentagon has become a complex institution that has ties to virtually every elected official whose "home state" wants cost overrun defense contracts. The military and its overseas adventures is also very popular among many voters but especially the white male dominated electorate. The U.S. middle class and working class understand well that their standard of living is tied to world domination. This creates the material conditions for their literal "buying in" to the lie that invasion of others is "self-defense." And now, with the Army and Marines reaching

---

16. Christopher Hellman, "Last of the Big Time Spenders," *Center for Defense Information*, 4 February 2002.

out to inner city youth of color, asking them to "Be all you can be," they are expanding the net of support for blind patriotism. The Pentagon, well aware of the mutinies and rebellions of many Black and Latino soldiers in Vietnam, is relying even more on aerial bombardment and demoralization of "enemy" civilians and soldiers in an effort to cut down on U.S. casualties.

But now, the Bush Administration is proposing a further escalation in violation of every international law, "the new strategic doctrine of pre-emption." As Richard Falk, a professor of law at UC Santa Barbara explains,

> The radical idea touted by the White House and Pentagon is that the United States has the right to use military force against any state that is seen as hostile or makes moves to acquire weapons of mass destruction—nuclear, biological, or chemical. This new approach repudiates the core idea of the United Nations charter (reinforced by the decisions of the World Court in the Hague) which prohibits any use of international force that is not undertaken in self-defense after the occurrence of an armed attack across an international boundary or pursuant to a decision by the UN Security Council. It is a doctrine without limits, without accountability to the UN or international law, without any dependence on a collective judgement of responsible governments, and what is worse, without any convincing demonstration of practical necessity.[17]

Unfortunately, there is practical necessity. The Bush Doctrine, including the threat of a nuclear first-strike, is part of a desperate international strategy that accepts no contending forces, no tolerance of any international challenges to U.S. rule.

---

17. Richard Falk, "The New Bush Doctrine," *The Nation*, July 15, 2002.

The threat of a nuclear first-strike continues to work to the advantage of the U.S. superpower by fostering the consciously cultivated image of the U.S. as a slightly mad, rogue bully.

Now that the Bush Administration has targeted Iraq, Iran, North Korea, Palestine, Venezuela, Cuba, and virtually every other nation in the world, we can better understand why the U.S. has an insatiable need for an infinite military buildup against an infinite number of identified enemies.

SECTION TWO
SO WHERE DO WE GO FROM HERE?
A MOVEMENT THAT DOES NOT YET EXIST IN SEARCH OF ANALYSIS, STRATEGY, AND TACTICS

When many of us were still in Durban, as WCAR was winding to a halt, the questions were raised, how would we bring back the lessons of the conference to the United States? How can we possibly plan a systematic resistance? In those conversations, many U.S. NGO delegates were painfully frank about the weak state of the U.S. movement, the many internal contradictions within each ethnic and racial group, the conflicts among and between people of color, the challenges of white chauvinism among even antiracist white groups and people, and even more, the absence of a sense of common strategy, tactics, and movement. It was as if we wished for a different future historical period, but we didn't know how to usher one in. The recounting of the strategic assessments of the Bush Administration and the overall bipartisan imperialist strategy is certainly depressing, seen in isolation, issue by issue, abuse by abuse. But all together, it leads to a vision of an overextended empire, seemingly impervious to the possible impacts of its actions, or rather, making calculated assessments that in each instance its bullying, domination, and subjugation of others is in its class interests and those of the system. Perhaps. But the following discussion, which will end again with the importance of WCAR and the South African struggle, can contribute to debates about the direction of work for the antiracist Left.

The system is overextended, parasitic, and out of control—that is its strength and that is its weakness. It is fundamentally unstable and vulnerable but undeniably ferocious. Thomas Friedman, a right-wing *New York Times* columnist, praised George W. Bush for acting (or being) a little bit crazy, saying that his apparent mental instability would strike fear into the hearts of equally crazy and unstable "terrorists." "Meet Don Rumsfeld—he's even crazier than you," Friedman boasts to "the axis of evil." "There is a lot about the Bush team's foreign policy I don't like, but their willingness to be as crazy as some of our enemies is one thing they have right."[18] We know a system is in crisis when the Madness of King George is now held up as a tactical advantage.

Karl Marx spent decades in the British Museum in London studying the workings of capitalism because he believed that every successful revolution must be based on analyzing the "objective conditions" of the system, that is, the actions and dynamics of the system that a social movement cannot control. He then applied this analysis to the development of a strategy for

---

18. Thomas L. Friedman, "Crazier Than Thou," *New York Times*, 13 February 2002.

revolutionary action. Obviously, or it should be obvious, an antiracist, anti-imperialist united front cannot be built simply by analyzing how capitalism unfolds. It involves the most active intervention to change history. Still, analyzing the strengths and weaknesses of the system we are trying to change, transform, or replace, and understanding the potential for accelerating its contradictions, is essential.

In this instance, we see imperialism being carried away with itself, each time requiring more and more desperate measures to prop itself up economically and politically, even if those actions jeopardize its long-term stability. Right now the U.S. is financing its war against the world by super-exploiting the entire world, subjecting more than three billion people to abject poverty—that is, half the world's population is living on less than two dollars a day.[19]

The U.S. is cutting its own social programs at home, once a structural source of stability, getting rid of civil rights legislation 100 years in the making, and attacking the Bill of Rights and constitutional separation of church and state. Even more than Gingrich's announced counter-revolution, the Bush/Cheney crowd is moving to undermine the efforts at system stabilization that the U.S. ruling class—through Franklin Delano Roosevelt, Lyndon Johnson, and Jimmy Carter—tried to impose. Can the U.S. really dominate virtually every nation in the world? Can it pull off being the world's policeman? At what cost and for how long? Can the U.S. pull out of every international treaty, from Kyoto to the International Criminal Court? Can it abuse its de-

---

19. United Nations, "Poverty and the Millennium Development Goals," media fact sheet for the World Summit on Sustainable Development.

pendent European allies and force them to dismantle their own social welfare states? Can it support or create right-wing juntas throughout the Third World without any world revolutionary movement in response? Will the U.S. overproduce oil and cars until all of Antarctica melts and the small island states are truly flooded to death? Can it deregulate its stock market and then try to patch it up with band-aid legislation while moving to legally impose a selective but potent police state against any form of dissent at home? Can it continue to imprison two million people, and initiate surveillance of 19 million immigrants? Can it do so without any substantial mass resistance? I don't think so.

It is obvious that in the short-run the contradiction between the power of imperialism on the one hand and the general weakness of the international anti-imperialist forces on the other gives imperialism the dominant and defining role. But in the realm of analysis and long-term strategy, the U.S. imperialist system is in danger. In its desperate pursuit of declining profits, it is resorting to the madness that accompanies imperialism's decay. As we wrote in *Toward a Program of Resistance*, the empire is eating the world and itself alive. This should be clear, even if the path to an alternative is not.[20]

In a period of right-wing ideological assault against the Left, re-establishing centers of left counterhegemonic thought become strategically essential. One of the strengths of the system is its portrayal of "public opinion" as monolithic. A few days after September 11, as Bush was about to give his first speech reassuring the nation of U.S. power and commitment to retribution, he went "across the aisle" to hug fellow Democrats, a moving

---

20. *Toward a Program of Resistance*, "Problems of Imperialism," 6

sign of unity among several hundred of the most powerful and most corrupt white men in the world. The goal: to convey the illusion that "we" are "all" "for" "the war." But who are we? Black and white, Latino, Asian/Pacific Islander, and Indigenous, women and men, queer and straight. Is there really a "we" and are "we" all really for the war? What does it mean to be "for" the war, anyway? For wiretapping? For bombing of civilians? For propping up every failing business while the poor are thrown out on the street thanks to welfare reform? For the invasion of Iraq? For the Israeli attacks on the Palestinian refugee camps? For the rounding up of immigrants? For merging the CIA and FBI to spy on whom?

One theory of how to build opposition to war is to find self-interested angles first, that is, to focus on the violation of democratic rights "at home" or the Enron scandal or attacks on immigrants and then build on that to oppose U.S. efforts to seize all the world's oil resources and inflict a war on the world. But that view of incremental consciousness-raising, of seeking the self-interested angle, ignores the historical failure of that view in trying to organize inside an empire. Many outraged investors will yell, "Put the corporate crooks in jail" but in the next breath say, "Kill Osama bin Laden and Saddam Hussein." Many white liberals who support "democratic rights at home" argue, "We can kill 'the enemy' and invade other countries without violating our 'American' rights." Some Arab American groups have tried to stop the violations of their civil rights by reassuring the Bush Administration of how much they support the bombing of Afghanistan, essentially arguing, "Violate their rights, not ours; we are 'loyal Americans.'" Some Black people in the U.S. have been caught up in a patriotic frenzy. They appreciate seeing Colin and Condoleezza leading the war charge and want so badly to belong. How should we organize them? We can argue that the war is stealing funds from urgently needed social programs. This is certainly true, but, again, this is a narrow self-interest approach that won't work. Many of these same people would not fight to stop the attacks on welfare mothers, Black youth unjustly imprisoned, or parents fighting school vouchers, let alone fight against a war that gives them a chance to show their loyalty to the country.

By contrast, an antiracist, anti-imperialist Left might start with the slogan that some Black nationalist street orators yelled out to a crowd of passersby in midtown Manhattan, "You can't be patriotic on stolen land." It could build on Vijay Prashad's argument that the September 11 attacks were a direct result of the Clinton/Bush counterinsurgency strategy, "made in the U.S.A.," or begin with the courageous arguments of progressive relatives of those who died at the World Trade Center, "Not in my name." If one of the strengths of the system is its creation of the illusion of unanimity, then building centers of aggressive, defiant, left intellectual resistance is a key tactic in the struggle. In that racism and imperialism are at the heart of the U.S. ideological framework, antiracism and anti-imperialism are the central ideological concepts of contestation, the essence of counterhegemonic political education work.[21]

As just one example of ideological contestation, the Labor/Community Strategy Center is set up as a "think tank/act tank" because we believe that any effort to try to rebuild a Left needs a multiracial center where organizers can experiment with new

---

21. Program Demand Group, *Toward a Program of Resistance* (Los Angeles: AhoraNow Commentary Series, 2002) Lian Hurst Mann, Editor, available from www.AhoraNow.org.

ideas. In 1993, we initiated the "Billions for Buses; Fight Transit Racism" campaign, challenging the racism of L.A.'s public transportation system. At the time, many white progressives, in particular, challenged us, "Why do you have to call it racism, the bus system is broken down for 'everyone.'" Even a few passengers of color raised concerns, "We should stop talking about racism, the system treats us like we want a handout when we talk about it." We replied that 90 percent of the passengers are Black, Latino, and Asian/Pacific Islander The system *is* racist, and that slogan helps us organize our key constituency—Black, Latino, Asian/Pacific Islander women and men, the lowest-income people. We also welcome that debate within communities of color. We understand very well that there is no unanimity of thought based on race. Over time, we have been able to attract a relatively large constituency of oppressed nationality bus riders as well as truly progressive whites who came to the Bus Riders Union because of our strong antiracist line. And yet, the Los Angeles MTA hates us because of our accusations of racism. Governmental officials, including Black and Latino board members scream at us, "Stop talking about racism, that's all you ever say." That's not true. We say many things, but that's the line that they hear most clearly. We see that racism is the system's Achilles heel.

Shortly after the September 11 events, several young Bay Area Leftists began to use the Malcolm X expression, "The chickens have come home to roost." They were immediately chastised by several prominent Leftists to be careful about making "left errors," that is, to not go too far ahead of the actual historical situation and its possibilities, and to refrain from using incendiary rhetoric that would turn off many working people and bring repression down on a fledgling left resistance. Certainly, at a time of mass patriotic hysteria, the use of inappropriately provocative and dogmatic slogans is not a good idea, but in this case, I think the young revolutionaries, mainly women and people of color, were onto something.

When Malcolm X first used the expression, "the chickens have come home to roost" he was referring to the assassination of John F. Kennedy. It was assumed that he was simply being vindictive, but his point was that the U.S. was built on the basis of murder, and that, in particular, Kennedy had willingly used the tactic of assassination himself, with the Green Berets in Vietnam and in his failed efforts to assassinate Fidel Castro. But this was 1963, when the Black Liberation Movement was just moving towards greater radicalism and militancy. Malcolm's statement was calculated to shake up Black people, white people, all people of color, to force a hard look at things that others did not want to face. It was a tactical move consistent with his own broader strategy of building an anti-imperialist wing of the Black Liberation Movement that would break with patriotism and take its issues to the United Nations and other international arenas.

Many people who were not active during the sixties, many who were active but have lost much of their revolutionary zeal, and many who were not even born yet, look back at "the sixties" as if something magical happened, which it did. Still, many people don't understand that it emerged, through struggle, in an earlier period involving a war against the conservative Cold War and the McCarthy witch hunt climate of the 1950s, a war of position in which ideology was a critical weapon. It was the work of specific individuals and groups who used very militant rhetoric to agitate their own core group—the most oppressed—who, we see in retrospect, built a militant grassroots base and were able to move history forward. SNCC's "Hell No, We Won't Go," the anti-war chant, "LBJ, LBJ, How Many Kids Did You Kill Today?", King's "The worst purveyor of violence in the world is my own government," and Malcolm's "The Ballot or the Bullet," and "The Farce on Washington," were powerful counterhegemonic slogans. Obviously, these are very difficult times, and the formulation of slogans must be done very carefully, but while caution is in order, so is some boldness and vitality. Counterhegemonic demand development is key: cut off all U.S. aid to Israel; support Palestinian self-determination; cut, don't expand the Pentagon budget; open borders, full political rights for immigrants; no to the police state at home and abroad; free the U.S. two million, release the prisoners from the racist jails; reparations for Africans, U.S. Blacks, and those in the African Diaspora, the U.S. must pay for its "crimes against humanity" in the Trans-Atlantic Slave Trade; no aggression against Iraq; stop the blockade of Cuba![22]

If you try to remember the most influential person, the most influential idea that changed your life, did you really agree with her or his ideas the first time you heard them? Or were you shaken up, agitated, and threatened as your previous belief system came under frontal attack? Were you challenged, transformed over time and moved to another place of consciousness that involved rejecting a previous world view, not just a previous opinion? How do we find a discourse that is respectful of our constituency, but not comfortable, and certainly not operating within the system's rules? We need a period of experimentation

---

22. See *Toward a Program of Resistance*, "Components of Our Approach to Demand Development," 7.

in developing jarring agitation. We need a strong, assertive, aggressive challenge to the entire system, to push back on the rightward madness while we can. We need to change minds, to break the dictatorial illusion of unanimity, which in turn will allow others to say, "I thought I was the only one who didn't support this war" and to keep open the space for dissent by building a popular movement, rooted in key communities and constituencies, that the government will have difficulty repressing.

Reparations Is the Ultimate Counterhegemonic Demand

The power of the Reparations Movement lies in its character as a radical reform demand. It can never be won fully, and the U.S. can never pay its full debt, unless the U.S. ceases to exist. Yet many concrete components of demands can be won and can create a foundation for even more structural demands, rather than close off future demands. In Durban, we saw many African writers, scholars, activists, organizers, and even several African governments condemning the entire history of Western barbarism that called itself civilization. How do we talk about a genocide that began in the 1400s and continues, in effect, today? How do we talk about the stealing, raping, mutilating, and degrading of an entire people and an entire continent for centuries? How do we talk about Christian white Europeans designing slave ships with tiny cubicles so efficiently designed that there was not an extra inch for each transported Black slave, knowing full well that many of the "cargo" would die in the Middle Passage? The more we examine the slave trade, the more grotesque the story becomes, the more pervasive, the more fundamental to every fiber of U.S. and European society. It calls for the most revolutionary reparations.

The movement for reparations was able to put the United States, the most powerful nation in the world, on the defensive in Durban. The U.S. was so worried about a mass condemnation of its history, that it had to flee the scene. The fight for reparations has the potential to challenge the entire ideological structure of the present right-wing juggernaut.

Reparations and the Black Liberation Movement

The struggle for reparations can help the Black Left and the Black working class rebuild its leadership in a broad united front for national self-determination. Since the great victories of the 1950s through 1970s, the U.S. Black Liberation Movement has been in a state of disorientation and decline. The causes require the most thoughtful historical analysis and interpretation, but one component to further investigate is the growing class split among Black people, and the development of a Black bourgeoisie that has abandoned the Black working class. Further, the Black working class has had particular difficulty developing its own independent class and race politics. This would require a greater focus on the class struggle among Black people in a way to strengthen the multi-class united front for Black liberation but to do so in a way that Black working class politics would have more influence on the programmatic direction of the movement. Such a class politics would emphasize the unique demands of Black workers that can actualize their critical strategic role as leadership of both the national liberation movement of Black people and the multiracial, multinational U.S. working class struggle.

The struggle for reparations will require an important alliance—a united front—between Black intellectuals, professionals, lawyers, and the masses of Black working class people. And from that oppressed nationality foundation, it can reach out to build a multiracial base of support. Reparations, as all its progressive advocates argue, must go beyond (or, in some arguments, must exclude) cash payments to each individual Black person in order to claim, from the government and the corporations, the most long-term (that is, centuries of) material and ideological repair. The U.S. government must fund ideological transformation programs that will focus on mass public education, the rewriting and publicizing of the history of the slave trade, from high school and college courses to public education campaigns requiring compulsory radio and television coverage, led by Black scholars and reparations scholars chosen by the movement, not the system.

There is a need for the most generous and systematic social programs, including massive improvements in public schools, funding for the Historically Black Colleges and Universities, hospitals, medical centers, public transportation systems, income maintenance programs, as well as the radical overhaul of the criminal justice system beginning with the freeing of all prisoners incarcerated by racism and national oppression. As Charles Ogletree, co-chair of the Reparations Coordinating Committee observed, "The Reparations Movement must therefore focus on the poorest of the poor—it must finance social recovery for the bottom stuck, providing an opportunity to address comprehensively the problems of those who have not substantially benefited from integration or affirmative action."[23]

---

23. Charles Ogletree, "Litigating the Legacy of Slavery," New York Times, 31 March 2002.

Rebuilding Alliances Among Peoples of Color Based on the Specificity and Strategic Centrality of the Black Liberation Struggle

The movement for reparations for the sufferings of slavery will, in fact, build the overall antiracist movement. Structural benefits for Blacks—better public schools, hospitals, and housing—if won, will benefit all people of color and all working people. Such reparations must be centered on the Trans-Atlantic Slave Trade, not on "racism" toward people of color in a homogenized form. For a successful multiracial movement to be reconstructed, each ethnic, racial, and national group must have its own voice, its own program, and its own interests in the broader antiracist united front. The U.S. must respond to the specific atrocities of slavery—the denial of the right to read, the attacks on the Black family, the rape, castration, lynching and other forms of brutality with the specific objective of terrorizing and, thereby, hyper-exploiting, an entire culture and people. During the 1960s, most young revolutionaries of all races, when asked how they were radicalized, talked about the Black and Vietnamese movements, and many Latino and Asian/Pacific Islander revolutionaries traced their roots directly to SNCC, CORE, and the Black Panthers. We must recognize that the specific history of Blacks in the U.S. calls for a specific role for the Black Liberation Movement in the larger movement against national oppression and racism. Out of such dynamics of solidarity and rallying around Black and African demands for reparations, there is the possibility of *greater* unity among people of color.

Back to Africa

In Durban, we saw the power of the strategic alliance of the Black Liberation Movement and the African Liberation Movement. Right now, African nations are in grave trouble, with many military dictatorships replacing formerly vibrant democracies, with profound neoliberal penetration by transnational corporations, and with encroachments on their sovereignty by the U.S. and G8, working through the WTO and other U.S.-dominated institutions to literally shove agreements against African interests down their throats. The ravages of colonialism are still open sores. The genocide in Rwanda against the Tutsis was a brutal African against African atrocity, but it was rooted in centuries of tribal conflicts instigated by the Belgian colonialists. The AIDS pandemic is so frightening that even the most dedicated public health advocates in Africa can only propose a level of massive intervention and medical aid that would take a revolution in itself; yet ultimately, it must be understood as a manifestation of colonial genocide. The ANC has begun using the term "African pessimism" to mean a dynamic in which the former colonial powers, the U.S. and EU, are "writing off" the African continent. The African nations need more solidarity from the U.S. Black Liberation Movement and the broad antiracist movement. They are fighting for their lives. Just as the struggle against Apartheid galvanized that alliance for decades, the struggle for reparations can shape the next long period in history.

I attended an Environmental Justice Conference, sponsored by Dr. Robert Bullard and others at Clark Atlanta University in 1997. We were addressed by Dr. Owen Wiwa, the brother of Ken Saro-Wiwa, the heroic environmental leader of the Ogoni people, an oppressed group inside Nigeria, who was hanged for his opposition to the disastrous environmental policies in Nigeria of Shell Oil (many of whose arch henchmen sit in the Nigerian government, including its delegation to the United Nations). Dr. Wiwa said how happy he was to see a predominantly Black audience, because, until then, most of the students willing to fight for the Ogoni people on the campuses he visited were white. While he greatly appreciated their help and in fact felt their support was critical, he lamented the lack of significant Black involvement in many solidarity movements in Africa, where such an international alliance could have so much power.

Many of us who attended the World Conference Against Racism and its many meetings, panels, and demonstrations on reparations hope these discussions will bring together a Pan-African politics on reparations, uniting Blacks in Africa, the U.S. and the African Diaspora. From that solid base, a movement for reparations can reach out to people of good will of all races to build the broadest possible united front. Such an alliance can also provide support within the U.S. to challenge many of the worst U.S. governmental abuses in Africa and provide venues in the U.S. for African dissidents to visibly express their views.

Rebuilding the Antiracist White Tradition

The Reparations Movement can once again place the ideology of white supremacy in the United States back on the defensive. No more disgusting critiques of "political correctness" or Blacks "playing the race card." The focus on building the Reparations Movement, the gift of Durban, is not an attack on white people but an ideological and programmatic challenge to a capitalist, imperialist country whose very history and very existence depends on slavery, genocide, and white supremacy. This challenge can cause a necessary and strategic split among whites, just as it did in the Civil Rights Movement, in which whites were recruited, and challenged to decide, "Which side are you on?," "You're either part of the problem, or part of the solution." The Reparations Movement offers the opportunity for a multiracial movement in which white students, white intellectuals, and white workers can help make an investigation into the history of slavery and its legacy in every corporation, every university, every state, city, and town, every museum, every church, and every synagogue, and yes, every family—accounting for the abuses committed and the structural and tangible benefits that were reaped from the lives and labor of Black slaves.

Reparations, of course, will shake the U.S. body politic to its foundations. The nation as we know it now would cease to exist. I remember working in an auto factory in the early 1980s when the *Roots* television series was first shown. I listened as an angry white worker began to rant, "Why do they have to show that stuff that is from so long ago, I didn't do anything to those people, I'm not a racist, and I'm not a slave owner." I responded, "You sure are acting like one. What do you have to hide?" Most white people know that the slave trade and the centuries of genocide against Blacks are deeply ingrained in white culture and the dominant capitalist society. Most white people know that the U.S. was built upon genocide against the Indigenous peoples and an entire economy and culture constructed upon a foundation of slavery. Most white people know that the myth of "white supremacy" is based on crimes against humanity, and that white people have benefited both psychologically and materially from white supremacy.

During the 1950s and 1960s, the Black Liberation Movement became more "nationalistic," that is, it focused on the *structural* basis of Black experience as an oppressed people. In many cases, the strategic alliance with antiracist whites became even more critical, as many white liberals abandoned the cause. There is a long history of militant and courageous antiracist white actions, from John Brown to the many foreign-born communists in the Scottsboro defense, to the courageous Andy Goodman and Mickey Schwerner, to an entire generation of white students who were an essential component of the Civil Rights Movement and a dependable ally of the Black Liberation Movement. These white activists and organizers broke with the dominant culture and went to war with the culture and institutions of white supremacy. Over the past decades, just as every other aspect of the movement has regressed, so has the antiracist consciousness of many progressive white people. Reparations, in many ways the most profound challenge to the entire structure of Western imperialism, offers the historical opportunity to reconstruct that important tradition, creating an essential strategic alliance between the Black Liberation Movement and the movements of all peoples of color in the United States and throughout the world.

Today, many dedicated young white people have been involved in the anti-globalization movement and movements against sweatshops, and have tried to fight both big business and global injustice. Often, their consciousness about racism and its structural ties to imperialism is not as strong as it could be, and sometimes their views are outright chauvinist. Part of the problem is the absence of a rigorous antiracist education on the part of white Leftists, and part is a product of the shortage of Black or Latino Left organizations forcing structural historical choices upon the broader society, which in turn would force young white activists to make harder choices, and give them opportunities to act. The Reparations Movement has the potential to provide a transformative vehicle in U.S. politics, and to create a split in the white electorate, and in the dominant white culture that can weaken the forces of white supremacy, strengthen the antiracist white forces, and strengthen the forces of Black self-determination and national liberation.

Reparations Threat to the Post-September 11 War Machine

The events of September 11 have indeed eclipsed some of the gains of the World Conference Against Racism. The power of this right-wing juggernaut has put virtually every social movement back on its heels, at least in the initial months. Now, as almost a year has passed, there is growing opposition to the right-wing agenda, but with little focus on a programmatic alternative. The Reparations Movement can provide a framework for a reconstructed antiracist, anti-imperialist Left in the United States. Imagine if the students at a high school decide they want to investigate all the prominent alumni and their ties to slavery, or have each student trace their roots to the period of slavery, or choose several key corporations in the area such as insurance companies, railroads, and manufacturers and do a corporate family tree, including tracing each merger back to the time of slavery. Imagine this movement really taking off, with Black students and parents turning this research into demands for a first class school system and massive investment of federal funds. Then imagine that you are investigating the Bush family from its roots at Yale and the CIA to its past racist practices and its ties to the Trans-Atlantic Slave Trade. Can you imagine, in that context, Bush coming in and arguing that as "loyal Americans" we should invade Iraq or North Korea, or round up all the immigrants?

The strategy proposed here proposes a direct struggle with the ideology of the Right, through the building of actual demands and programs in the working class and from there expanding to a broad united front. It tries to consolidate the urban centers—New York, Chicago, Atlanta, San Francisco/Oakland, New Orleans, Houston, Detroit, and Los Angeles, all with large Black, Latino, Asian/Pacific Islander, and immigrant populations, as centers of resistance to the permanent war machine. It looks for the most controversial, but organizable, demands around which we believe a movement can really be built. In that context, reparations plays an exciting and central role.

Palestinian Self-determination: A Profound Challenge on the World Stage

The Palestinian struggle since WCAR has been characterized by several new developments. First, if it seemed impossible for things to get worse, the murder of Palestinian civilians by heavily armed Israeli troops (paid for with U.S. military aid) has escalated. This is not meant at all to minimize the impact of Palestinian self-defense tactics of suicide bombings, aimed against civilians in the settlements and against the military infrastructure of the West Bank and Gaza Strip, but while some Palestinians have spoken out against the tactic, in fact no one has a better alternative. It is hard to figure out strategy and tactics in the midst of a campaign of Israeli annihilation of the Palestinian people. As Palestinians debate the best tactics among themselves, there must be an international movement to defend their right to self-defense, and to stay Israel's hand, before it is too late for everyone.

Second, the Bush Administration has used the "war against terrorism" to condemn all efforts at armed resistance and self-defense by forces with which it does not agree. Israeli mass murder and destruction in the Jenin refugee camp is called "unfortunate." Israeli use of U.S. missiles to assassinate Hamas leaders and kill children is deemed "heavy-handed" but acceptable. Palestinian armed counterattacks are treated with mock outrage, to encourage another round of Israeli troop invasions and re-occupation.

Third, and fortunately, international support for the Palestinians is growing in the U.S., Europe, and South Africa. While many Arab leaders, in trying to appease the U.S., have in fact done little to help the Palestinian cause, this does not account for the "Arab Street," the popular forces in each Arab nation state who support the Palestinians. In fact, the grassroots, militant stance of many Arabs in support of the Intifada has caused much conflict between Arab peoples and their governments. There is a growing boycott of both Israeli and U.S. products across the Arab world in protest of both countries' actions against Palestine.

The Bush/Sharon policy of "total war" against the Palestinians has validated the charges the Palestinians made in Durban, and made the connection between Israel, racism, and Apartheid even more pronounced, at least among some progressive audiences. Desmond Tutu, the former Anglican Bishop from South Africa, recently spoke out about "Apartheid in the Holy Land."

> In our struggle against Apartheid, the great supporters were Jewish people. I believe Israel has a right to secure borders. What is not so understandable, not justified, is what it did to another people to guarantee its existence. I've been very deeply distressed in my visit to the Holy Land; it reminded me so much of what happened to us Black people in South Africa. I have seen the humiliation of the Palestinians at checkpoints and roadblocks, suffering like us when young white officers prevented us from moving about... My heart aches. I say, why are our memories so short? Have our Jewish sisters and brothers forgotten their humiliation? Have they forgotten the collective punishment, the home demolitions, in their own history so soon? Israel will never get true security and safety through oppressing another people... Israel has three options: revert to the previous stalemated situation, exterminate all Palestinians, or—I hope—to strive for peace based on justice, based on withdrawal from all occupied territories, and the establishment of a viable Palestinian state on those territories side by side with Israel, both with secure borders.[25]

Tutu begins by calling out the Jewish people, not just the Israelis, on the grounds that the vast majority of Jews support the Israeli brutality. Tutu is challenging those who say that if you mention Jews and Israel together you are anti-Semitic (and, as he observes later in his speech, are not the Palestinians Semites as well?) Then he makes direct analogies to Apartheid and accuses Israel of being an occupying army. He later adds, "And how did it come about that Israel was collaborating with the Apartheid

---

25. Desmond Tutu, "Apartheid in the Holy Land," The Guardian, 29 April 2002.

government on security measures?" So, Israel is not just racist, but a "collaborator," one of the worst charges the anti-Nazi movement made against those who aided Hitler. Worse, Tutu warns the Israelis: Are you planning to exterminate the Palestinians? Tutu's polemic shows the struggle in Durban to be prophetic and illustrates how world events can change rapidly.

Israel is becoming an international pariah—a powerful one but a pariah nonetheless. Meanwhile, the Sharon regime, with the full support of Bush, is working toward a strategy to terrorize the Palestinian people, to break their will to exist and then to move in with the reactionary Arab states to impose a negotiated settlement that condemns the Palestinians to a future of neocolonial dependency, under Israeli and U.S. control.

Like Bush, the Israelis are pursuing a scorched earth diplomatic policy that says, "The hell with all allies." It is this political and diplomatic isolation that will contribute to Israel's ultimate implosion or its degeneration into a complete police state against its own people as well. The theme of capitalist overextension repeats itself, and the Palestinians, by their continued resistance, are forcing the Israelis, and the Bush Administration, into a strategic miscalculation that is gaining them, if this is possible, more and more enemies in the Arab world, enemies the U.S. cannot dismiss or control.

The fights for reparations and Palestinian self-determination are key components of an overall anti-imperialist strategy. At the Strategy Center, a project group called the Program Demand Group has spent more than a year developing a comprehensive antiracist, anti-imperialist document, *Toward a Program of Resistance*, in which 24 key demands situated in six major programmatic areas of emphasis are articulated, not as a blueprint, but as a methodological guide to demand development reflecting a coherent left strategy. In this historical period, reaching agreement on a common program of action will be crucial to bringing groups together and expanding the scope of the Left.

SECTION THREE
A PROGRAMMATIC OFFENSIVE
Defending the Right to Self-Determination and Revolution

Since Durban, the United States has been involved in a thus far unsuccessful effort to overthrow Venezuela's elected president, Hugo Chavez, has called for the Palestinians to oust Palestinian Authority leader Yasir Arafat, and has openly threatened invasion of Iraq, allegedly to remove its president, Saddam Hussein, unless the U.S. can assassinate him first. The ideology of empire, reflected in U.S. great nation chauvinism, is so deep in U.S. culture that significant numbers of white voters in particular think nothing of open plans to overthrow other people's governments and to assassinate their leaders, all in the name of "defense." Even Jimmy Carter's recent visit to Cuba, which the Cubans obviously saw as a split in the U.S. ruling class, was characterized by the most embarrassing social chauvinism, as the Peanut Farmer lectured the Cubans on human rights and the free market and even tried to support an opposition group within Cuba as a trade off for his opposition to the U.S. blockade.

At this point in history, counterhegemonic, transformative organizing must include, and prioritize, the defense of the right of self-determination of nations being threatened by

U.S. efforts to topple their leaders and social systems. Such invasions can be made more difficult if there is a vocal, viable opposition in the U.S., and most effectively, a pre-emptive one. A minority voice in the U.S. that opposes specific abuses of the empire can be very influential, because the system runs with the hope of no public debate, as both political parties conspire to limit the bounds of thinkable thought. A movement to pre-emptively oppose the invasion of Iraq would be one example of a tactical intervention by the Left based on this strategy.

In the next decade, the U.S. will continue its plan to literally overthrow governments and, if possible, set up puppet regimes all over the world. That is nothing new. What would be new would be an organized opposition inside the U.S. to create an open political debate, and at best, a split in popular opinion that could stay the hand of the U.S. army and CIA and strengthen the sovereignty and self-determination, including their right to social revolution, of oppressed nations throughout the world.

There is reason for hope. While the dominant ideology of U.S. society is slavish support of empire, there is, in fact, a strong anti-imperialist tradition, often not expressed in such ideological terms, but still in open disagreement with and opposition to particular abuses of the U.S. government. After the September 11 events, while some on the Left bit their tongues, afraid to appear "ultra-left" at a time of mass suffering, several families of those killed at the World Trade Center exercised courage and audacity.

Amber Amundson lost her husband Craig in the Pentagon. She wrote in the *Chicago Tribune*, "If you choose to respond to this incomprehensible brutality by perpetuating violence against any other innocent human beings, you may not do so in the name of justice for my husband."

Matthew Lasar praised his uncle, Abe Zelmanowitz, who stood by a quadriplegic friend in the World Trade Center rather than flee the building and who died in the fire. Taking sharp issue with California Senator Dianne Feinstein's statement, "Whether that entity is a state or an organization, those who harbor them, arm them, train them, and permit them must, in my view, be destroyed," Lasar responded, "How does one destroy states? Through the covert subversion of their societies? Through carpet-bombing? Afghanistan has more than a million homeless refugees. A U.S. military intervention could result in the starvation of tens of thousands of people. What I see are actions and policies that will cost many more innocent lives, and breed more terrorism, not less. I do not feel that my uncle's compassionate heroic sacrifice will be honored by what the U.S. appears poised to do."[26]

During the movement against the war in Vietnam, there were everyday acts of heroism by anti-war protestors. People, including many Black and Latino youth, risked their lives, many going to jail rather than "serve" others. Many engaged in militant resistance once drafted into the army, others fled to Canada, and still others risked their jobs and families to speak out. Many white students threw their bodies in front of the military at the Pentagon and Kent State, with "four dead in Ohio" serving as martyrs to the cause. It will take workers in factories circulating signed petitions refusing to attack civilians, leaflets at army bases urging Black and Latino GIs to refuse to become an occupying army in the Third World, and campaigns to expose the serial mi-

---

26. "Not in Our Names: Relatives of September 11 Attacks Speak Out," Institute for Public Accuracy press release, 27 September 2002.

sogyny of the soldiers who returned to Fort Bragg to murder their wives—what kind of madness is the Bush Administration inflicting upon this country?

The International Importance of the U.S. Anti-imperialist Left

From the 1940s to the 1970s, the Third World revolutionary movements for self-determination and socialism helped greatly in the development of the Black Liberation Movement and helped people of color win enormous gains in the U.S. Today the Third World both inside and outside the U.S. is under profound attack. The U.S. Left, even if it does not yet exist in any coordinated or formalized form, must come together in defense of a Third World that our own government is driving over the edge of poverty, pollution, and recolonization.

At the height of the war in Vietnam, there were demonstrations against the war that were truly amazing to behold. I remember a large anti-war mobilization in New York in 1966. I was standing on a pre-arranged street corner on Fifth Avenue, waiting for a friend who told me he would be marching with "Teachers Against the War." As I stood on the corner, first for ten minutes, then twenty, then over an hour, thousands upon thousands of people marched by me, each with their banners: "Dewitt Clinton High School Against the War;" then "Women;" then "Black Liberation Movement;" then each civil rights group; then Yonkers, the Bronx, Brooklyn, Queens, Jamaica, and even Staten Island; then Bedford Stuyvesant and Harlem; and then even "Psychiatrists Against the War" who felt Johnson should get his head examined. At the time, I had no idea how much those marches meant to the Vietnamese people, but I did know how much the Vietnamese meant to us. They were fighting for their own national liberation but also for the humanity of those of us who live in the heart of the empire, in the heart of imperialist darkness.

It is not clear what significance will be given to the World Conference Against Racism, for, in all history, it is the responsibility of the participants to shape the historical record—to study history by making history. This book makes the strategic assessment that WCAR was already very important, and has the potential to go down in history as a turning point in the world movement against racism. If the U.S. Reparations Movement alone holds that view, it can become a self-fulfilling prophesy. For those who see despair in the present situation, a long historical lens is needed. Desmond Tutu observed, warning both Israel and the United States, "We live in a moral universe. The Apartheid government was very powerful, but today it no longer exists. Hitler, Mussolini, Stalin, Pinochet, Milosevic, and Idi Amin were all powerful, but in the end they bit the dust."[27]

It is hard to see the George W. Bush/Democratic Party war machine as vulnerable, and yet, they are sowing the seeds of their own destruction—asking for voluntary participation in a U.S. police state and enthusiastic support for a war that they inform us will never end. In fact, the system is choking on its own avarice and creating many forces in the world that see the United States as the main aggressor in the world. Eventually, those oppressed forces must come together. This book is a small tactic

---

27. Desmond Tutu, "Apartheid in the Holy Land."

in the larger strategy of reconstructing a world antiracist Left, a world united front against imperialism.

As we train people to go out organizing on the bus, we assure them, "You are not there to get people angry. They should already be angry about the conditions on the bus, the conditions of their life. You should not be giving speeches *at* people but talking *to* people, explaining your own politics in a passionate and persuasive manner that can encourage others, if they agree, to join us." One of our new slogans is, "We are looking for the people who are looking for us." Denise Fay Hall, a young Black woman who had been going to school in a virtually all-white, and apparently all-Right college, was one such member we recruited on the bus. She is now an organizer-in-training at our National School for Strategic Organizing. Explaining her own radicalization, she said, "I kept hearing about the Right, the Right. I figured, there must be a Left somewhere!"